W9-AUG-305

HAVE A NICE DAY

FROM THE BALKAN WAR TO THE AMERICAN DREAM

Dubravka Ugrešić

Translated by Celia Hawkesworth

JONATHAN CAPE
LONDON

First published in the United Kingdom in 1994

1 3 5 7 9 10 8 6 4 2

© Dubravka Ugrešić 1993
Translation © Celia Hawkesworth 1994

Dubravka Ugrešić has asserted her right
under the Copyright, Designs and Patents Act 1988
to be identified as the author of this work

First published in the United Kingdom in 1994 by Jonathan Cape
Random House, 20 Vauxhall Bridge Road, London SW1V 2SA

Random House Australia (Pty) Limited
20 Alfred Street, Milsons Point, Sydney,
New South Wales 2061, Australia

Random House New Zealand Limited
18 Poland Road, Glenfield,
Auckland 10, New Zealand

Random House South Africa (Pty) Limited
PO Box 337, Bergvlei, South Africa

Random House UK Limited Reg. No. 954009

A CIP catalogue record for this book
is available from the British Library

ISBN 0–224–03885–0

Printed in Great Britain by
Mackays of Chatham plc, Chatham, Kent

So, gentlemen, you would like me to show you the house where I was born? But I came into the world in a hospital in Fiume and that hospital has been pulled down. You will not be able to put a plaque on the house where I lived, for it too has probably been pulled down. Or you could put up three or four plaques with my name on them in various towns and various countries, but I wouldn't be able to help there either, because I no longer remember where I lived as a child, I hardly know which language I spoke. What I do remember are images: a palm waving and oleanders somewhere by the sea. The murky green Danube flowing past meadows, a counting rhyme: eenie-meenie-minie-mo . . .

Danilo Kiš, fragment from the unfinished
story 'The Man Without a Country'

CONTENTS

MY AMERICAN FICTIONARY

Every book has its own personal story of coming into being. It remains hidden from the reader and usually has meaning only for the author. Sometimes, however, it is hard to separate the story of its coming into being from the book itself, sometimes the story of its making *is* the book itself.

I wrote this book at a time when 'all my words had scattered', just like those of Lewis Carroll's Alice. By writing I have tried to put my scattered words (and scattered worlds) into some sort of order. That, I think, is why I originally called it *My American Dictionary*. Because only words which have been put in order can be tidied away in dictionaries.

I spent September 1991, with my fellow citizens of Zagreb, in the cellar of the block of flats where I live. War had begun in my country. In accordance with the instructions of the Bureau for Civil Defence, we all kept beside the door 'a bag of the most essential items'. At the sound of the air-raid warning siren we would all run down to our cellars, improvised shelters, carrying those bags with us. Many women carried needles and wool and spent the time knitting!

At the end of September I was invited to Amsterdam. Throwing some clothes into the 'bag of the most essential items', I boarded the train on a day when there were no air-raid warnings. At the beginning of January the following year I was supposed to go to Wesleyan University in Middletown, Connecticut. But at that stage America seemed about as far away as another planet.

Instead of the proposed week in Amsterdam, I stayed for three. Every day I would set off for the station and then postpone my return to Zagreb with the firm intention of leaving the following day ... These postponements betrayed a childish disbelief, the hope that the war was just a nightmare which would vanish in the morning as though it had never been.

And then I suddenly decided that I would not go back. And it was as though it was not I who had made the decision but fear mixed with despair, despair with hopelessness, hopelessness with a vague sense of shame ...

In Amsterdam I applied for a visa and set off for America somewhat earlier than I was meant to. I didn't know then that horror can't be eliminated by moving away from it. The price of going away is two-fold fear: fear for one's family, friends, city, and for one's 'emotional property'. That seems to be the way things go. Everyone pays his price, no one gets by scot free.

While I was in Amsterdam I wrote a short piece for a Dutch daily newspaper. And when I reached America the paper offered me a regular column of 1,000 words. Without thinking much about it, I called the column 'My American Dictionary'. That little column saved my life.

How could a thousand words save a life? There was a time when I had a powerful sense of being NOWHERE. Even innocent Middletown (of which there are about thirty with the same name in America!) only increased my anxiety. Grabbing the slender Amsterdam commitment like a straw, I set up my inner coordinates in an empty space: Zagreb—Amsterdam—Middletown. What saves a life is a daily routine: putting paper into the typewriter, writing an article, sending it to Amsterdam, phoning Zagreb . . .

'Your articles are very sad: they seem to be about someone who has stumbled into a completely empty house and is now furnishing it with things, slowly and rather absent-mindedly,' Henk wrote somewhat later. Henk Figee is a writer, the editor of my Dutch books and a friend. I had no idea then that the image of 'someone who had stumbled into a completely empty house' would grow into a permanent sense of homelessness.

This is an indecent book. I have always believed (and I still do) that a writer with any self-respect should avoid three things:

a) autobiography

b) writing about other countries

c) diaries

All three smack of narcissism, which is undoubtedly the basic premise of any literary act, but ought not also to be its outcome. And in all three genres this outcome is hard to avoid.

I have always felt that writing about oneself was a kind of self-improvement exercise, a service of the cult of self, indecently tedious for everyone else. Writing about other countries is also a kind of disguised indecency; it not only implies a foolish belief that one's personal view of things is unique, but reduces the irreducible to little dead sheets of paper with writing on it. As for the diary genre, I used to believe it was just a forgivable sin of cultural growing-up. Sorrowful literary practice in my country demonstrates that the diary is, in fact, a war genre.

So, this book has been written against my personal and literary convictions. But excuses, of whatever kind, are always superfluous: this book belongs to genres a) and b) and c). This book is neither a) nor b) nor c). It was meant to be a book about one thing, it turned out to be a book about something else, and written for someone quite different. Even its author is uncertain. I now feel that it was not I who wrote it but some adult Alice, whose 'words had scattered', who didn't know who she was: one moment she thought that she was bigger than a house, the next so small that she could have drowned in a pool of tears.

At Wesleyan University I gave lectures in *English* on the Central European and East European novel, without really knowing what was Central and what Eastern Europe. I gave lectures in *Russian* on the literature of the Russian avantgarde. So it was that English Kundera was mixed up with Russian Pilnyak, Russian Hlebnikov with English Hrabal, English Danilo Kiš with Russian Daniil Kharms, and he with American everyday life. With Irka, a friend from Moscow, now an American citizen, I spoke Russian, evoking old, shared, Moscow memories. The parallel worlds, those past and these present ones, criss-crossed quite naturally.

I telephoned Zagreb often. My mother's voice poured out of the telephone receiver. In nervous disorder the daily prices of meat and lettuce in the Zagreb market were mixed up with the number of war casualties, with little bits of news about our neighbours and the refugees she had taken to live with her, with the news of the death of an old friend. On the telephone lines the sound of an air-raid siren merged with the names of the cosmetic frivolities she wanted me to send her. Make-up is terribly expensive, face cream is a quarter of my pension, said my mother, crying. Her tears expressed fear, humiliation, alarm, both awareness that in the midst of air-raid warnings she was asking for something quite meaningless, and a panic-stricken need for life to be what it had always been, all at the same time. I would go to the shop, choose face cream for my mother in *English*, thinking of her in *Croatian*. I would buy the little things she wanted as though that act would bring the war itself to an end.

I often called Maja in Ithaca, who called Hatidža in Sarajevo; I called Andrea in New Haven every day and she often called Igor in Osijek; I would call Goran in New York, who often called his mother in Mostar ... We called each other, exchanging news like war correspondents, thousands of miles from the front.

A further dimension — Amsterdam — was added to the exhausting mental and emotional simultaneity, the frenzied criss-crossing of parallel worlds. This was soothing, as had been my first sight of the Netherlands, as I arrived by the night train from Vienna into the Dutch morning: a picture of light-green meadows in a mist above which large, motionless cows floated like benign ghosts. At night, after I sent off my thousand words to Amsterdam, I often soothed myself to sleep with the poetic image of my white tubes of text springing like paper tulips out of the fax-machine into the early Amsterdam morning. The cleaning woman would contemplate my little tube of paper with sleepy surprise, not understanding the text, funny little blobs and squiggles, a 'message in a bottle' ...

All at once these worlds crossed and merged at an almost legitimate point, in the land on the other side of the looking-glass, in America. America was gradually moving into me, at times I accepted its tenancy with gratitude, at others I would shove it out. I did not yet know that in America I lived in — an inner shelter.

People in shelters quickly establish an appearance of normality, and indeed, at a certain time it seemed that things had never been any different. It was only unambiguous details that corrected this distorted perception. That 'bag of the most essential items' still stood by the door of my American flat.

This book is about all of that. So why did I originally call it a dictionary without thinking much about it? The word was part of my refugee luggage; the idea of a different kind of dictionary, which would probably never be written, travelled with me.

A year ago, sorting through some old things, I found my first reading primer, dated 1957. A whole world I had entirely forgotten was shaken out of the primer along with the dust. At that time walls, towns, borders — the whole world described by my primer — were vanishing. The names of streets were vanishing and being replaced by new ones, the names of squares and towns, photographs and encyclopaedia entries were disappearing, people were disappearing, a whole mythology was vanishing and being replaced by another, a country was disappearing and being replaced by another, an age half a century old was disappearing . . . Good or bad, right or wrong, that was the age in which we had lived: those were the letters we had learned, those were the books we had read, the objects we had possessed, the films we had watched, the streets we had walked. All of a sudden we had to change everything: addresses and address books, language and names, personal documents, identity . . . With astounding and unbelievable speed everything had been turned into a lumber-room, without anyone having had time to stick labels onto anything. A whole country had been condensed into an encyclopaedia entry and, like Atlantis, moved into the *Dictionary of Imaginary Places*.

I think now that in this postmodern age the increasingly common genre of the dictionary — which has abandoned its linguistic framework and moved over into literature — has less to do with nostalgia than might appear at first. The exercise of this form seems rather to resemble the effort of patients with Alzheimer's disease to find their way around with the help of little bits of paper, notelets, labels, before they (or the world?) sink into complete oblivion. All the various dictionaries in this postmodern age are only an intimation of the chaos of oblivion.

This book is about all of that. But still, why a dictionary? Perhaps it had grown out of the same vague fear that had driven my American student David Lehman to write the sentence, 'The world is fragile and I am afraid.' Or again perhaps it was the same passion, entirely inappropriate to the situation, with which the women in the shelters during the air-raid warnings had knitted pullovers and blankets, quite pointless things. No explanation seems sufficiently accurate now.

On my return to Zagreb at the end of June 1992, I had the impression that *reality no longer existed*. The state of my country, which was falling apart and vanishing, surpassed even the direst forebodings, erased the boundaries between existing and imaginary worlds, and I found myself once more on the wrong side of a looking-glass.

As I was retyping the texts of my American dictionary, I mistakenly typed **f** instead of **d**, and my dictionary became a fictionary. The chance mistake only confirmed my inner nightmare. Because if *reality no longer existed*, then both 'fiction' and 'faction' were losing their initial meaning. And the words I had collected in a heap had scattered again. Somewhere along the way I discovered what I had always known: that even an accidental mistake cannot be accidental because it is certain to have already come to life in some other place, some other language. And indeed, the French philosopher Alain Finkeilkraut treats his 'fictionary', his *Petit Fictionnaire Illustré*, as a store of those words which are just a stimulus, 'a pre-text for a story'.

In Zagreb I found myself once again in my inner shelter. The enormous misery, Sarajevo, Bosnia, was now throbbing at full strength. Caught in its rhythm, I began once again to sort through the scattered words. The intimate story of the genesis of a different book had begun.

I also discovered something I had not previously known. That pullover knitted in the shelter was a deeply subconscious act of self-defence, a way (the only one we know) of containing chaos, an act of white magic. Knitting a pullover, we seem subconsciously to be knitting up the reality that others are violently unravelling at the same time. But the difference between a pullover knitted

17

in normal times and one knitted in a shelter cannot and need not be visible to the eye of the observer.

These texts came into being in the order in which they appear in this book in Amsterdam, Middletown and New York between October 1991 and June 1992. The Appendix and this conclusion, serving here as an introduction, were included in the manuscript later — in August of the same year, in Zagreb.

REFUGEE

'Where are you from?' the young Flemish photographer asked, in the hope that his question would make my tense face relax.

'Zagreb,' I said.

'And where's that?' he said casually, chewing gum.

Really, where is that? In Croatia. In a country which does not yet exist. And where is that? In Yugoslavia. In a country which no longer exists. If the country does not exist, then what is happening there cannot, actually, be happening. There is no death, the flattened cities are no longer flattened, there are no casualties, the refugees have not abandoned their homes, and the crazed generals of the Yugoslav Army do not exist either. Everything is as peaceful as a fixed flashback. I am at home in Holland, I am The Flying Dutchman.

I no longer know who I am, nor where I am, nor whose I am,
my mother said a few days ago. That day we had rushed
into the cellar, the improvised air-raid shelter, for the
fifth time. Obediently following civil defence instructions, we took our identity documents with us so that
we could be tidily identified if we were bombed, and
not end up as mere anonymous corpses.

When they discovered that I was going to Amsterdam,
my neighbours said: And just you tell that Van Den
Broek what is going on here . . .

We were all sitting in the cellar of our block of flats.
My neighbours were knitting and doing crochet, draw-
ing their shattered nerves through the soothing skeins
of wool and thread.

'I'll tell him . . .' I barked.

They looked at me without a trace of doubt in their
eyes. Now — as I walk through the streets of Amsterdam — I know that all those pullovers, cardigans and
bedspreads they began will be finished and they will be
desperately knitting and crocheting new garments in the
dark cellar.

In the foyer of the 'Ambassador' hotel on the Heren-
gracht canal (where the reflections of buildings tremble
in the water like fruit jelly), I answer the journalist's
questions.

'To date more than three hundred protected cultural
monuments have been destroyed in Croatia. Bombing

Dubrovnik is a crime of the same order as bombing Venice, for instance.'

'Bombing Venice!' She was genuinely shocked. 'How terrible!'

In Artis, the Amsterdam zoo, I was watching the tranquil reptiles. In my head was a note from a Zagreb newspaper I had read before I left. A group of my fellow-nationals were sending an open letter to Pavarotti on the occasion of his recent concert for the protection of the tortoises of the Galapagos. 'Mr Pavarotti,' my countrymen wrote, 'the Croats are no less under threat. The Croats are tortoises from the Galapagos.'

'They shouldn't have done that,' an acquaintance had commented, 'pathos is counter-productive.'

I agreed. Death is counter-productive.

The Yugoslav papers are full of open letters. Open letters to Kundera, to Peter Handke, to Gyorgy Konrad ... Open letters are a war genre, a genre of extreme despair, envisaged as the public denunciation of another, in practice a public annunciation of one's own feelings. Open letters are an extremely unnatural and inappropriate genre: They are never read by the people they're addressed to, they are a form of public self-denigration by those who write them. During the war Yugoslav literature has become reduced to two genres: open letters and diaries.

Everything has become tasteless, out-of-place, a bad

joke, *poshlost'*, the untranslatable Russian word Nabokov used somewhere — recycled tawdriness.

Rivers of refugees set out from the bombed city of Vukovar. One woman managed somehow to reach her relations in Zagreb who by chance lived in Vukovar Street. Having avoided death in Vukovar, the woman went out the next day and was hit by a random grenade. Her death is a bad joke. Deaths are no longer counted in Yugoslavia. Lives are at a discount, both Serbs and Croats die for a song.

I telephone my mother in Zagreb. She's crying.

'Don't worry,' she mumbles through her tears, 'we're all crying. Our nerves are in pieces.'

In the Bodega Kayzer café I drink coffee and write down pairs of opposites. Right — left; organized — disorganized; democracy — democratic symbols as a substitute for democracy; civilized — primitive; legitimate — illegitimate; rational consciousness — mythic consciousness; facing the future — a necrophiliac preoccupation with the past; predictability — unpredictability; an orderly system of criteria and values — absence of system; individual consciousness — collective consciousness; citizen — nationality. I fill the left-hand column under the heading Western Europe, the right under Eastern Europe.

And suddenly I see that same Eastern Europe. It's sitting at my table, we look at each other as in a mirror. I see a neglected complexion, cheap make-up, an expression of condescension and defiance on its face. It wipes its lips with its hand, talks too loudly, gesticulates, raises its eyebrows. I see in its eyes a glint of simultaneous despair and cunning, I see a panic-stricken need to stop being a second-class citizen and become someone. My sister, my sad Eastern Europe.

In the Hoppe café, I am introduced to a Yugoslav woman with an English surname, acquired through a simple marital transaction. I catch her scent, she's 'one of us', the sort I recognize immediately. She wrote a book, 'a personal story': she found herself in Kuwait, and since she was there, why not write a book about it . . . My life before Kuwait, my life after Kuwait . . . My countrywoman prattled on. Twenty-five thousand copies in America, twenty thousand in Germany, twenty in England, twenty in Holland . . . Only the French weren't interested, the bastards . . . There was going to be a film, she said, based on her personal story. She evidently liked the word 'personal'.

'Why don't you write about Yugoslavia? There's a kind of "Kuwait" there as well,' I say.

'That's not my personal story,' she says swiftly. 'Besides, it wouldn't be profitable in media terms, it's not *marketable*.'

I understand her. Kuwait was her suddenly acquired ID card, she's not letting it out of her hands as long as there's life in it. Misfortune needs a good design too, a label and a market. If the war horrors in Croatia had been presented by an international fashion designer someone would have noticed them. As it is there's just a heap of deaths and misery 'down there', in the Balkans, unacceptable in marketing terms. And as soon as it's unacceptable to the market, it's morally and emotionally unacceptable as well.

In the *Volkskrant* I read the headline: *'Nieuw offensief federaal leger tegen Kroatie.'* I don't understand the language, but I get the message. Like Erisichstones, the King of Thessaly whom Demeter punished with permanent hunger, the Yugoslav Federal Army will first devour Croatia, then for lack of sustenance it will eat up the rest of 'Titoland' — the egg that hatched it. Finally, having eaten its own children, it will die in terrible torment, devouring itself. The country whose ideology until a short time ago proclaimed a happy future is now creating that future: a land of beggars and cripples.

While factories in the Balkans are labouring to produce lies, deaths and utter annihilation, neighbouring countries are producing protective filters of indifference. I understand that we, down there, are the shit of Europe, an awkward problem, a handicapped relation... I understand that Europe wants only pink, healthy, compatible members in its family, but isn't it all terrible, I say bitterly.

'Stop tormenting yourself,' says an Amsterdam colleague. 'You're not your country, for heaven's sake!'

'Unfortunately I am,' I say abruptly and I don't know whether that fact, as simple as the beer in the glass in front of me, should make me laugh or cry.

In the American Embassy in Amsterdam, the official coldly rejects the young man and girl in the queue in front of me.

'Get your visas in Zagreb,' she says.

'But the consulate is closed there,' they say.

'We don't know anything about that,' says the official, the tone of her voice putting an end to the whole case.

I get my visa immediately. I'm going to teach at an American university. Here you are, of course, good luck.

I feel ashamed. I'm a privileged refugee.

I walk through the streets of Amsterdam. In the Leidseplein I stop beside a group of people demonstrating against fast food. I stand there, I, an ex-Yugoslav, I, who no longer know who I am, nor where I am, nor whose I am. I buy a little package of fast food, winking at the swarthy assistant. There's no food without fast food, I say. He smiles, he's 'one of us', Third World, I recognize him by the expression of condescension and cunning on his face. I stand there, mingling with the warm crowd, holding in my hand the *Diary of Laura Palmer* which I've just bought. In my head flash pictures of my homeland so like Lynch's soap-noir . . . Except that the blood that is flowing is real. The young man beside me is holding a placard saying: STOP FAST FOOD.

And I take a felt-tip out of my handbag, I write a message on the inside cover of Laura's diary, the only paper I have. STOP THE WAR IN CROATIA. I hold up the cover, completely aware of my own insignificance, completely aware of the *fatal strategies* of the world. Mingling with the warm crowd, I give out my signal. I look at a glamorous advertisement on the other side of the street. It winks at me as though it were saying: I'll think about that tomorrow. *I'll think about that tomorrow,* whispers my sister, my beautiful Western Europe.

ID

Before we boarded the plane for New York, the young official checked our passports again.

'I've never seen one of these!' he said, smiling.

'You may never see another,' I said, taking my passport and blushing at my sudden impudence, my impropriety, my tone which called anyone who was not *au fait* with the case to order, a tone which was deeply out of character but which had entered my voice, like a virus. I blushed at the tone which rang with the whole of my country, my Atlantis.

In the plane I began to shiver at the finality of my decision. The thought of going back was unbearable. The thought of being anywhere else was equally unbearable. I was incompatible. Over there. And over here. And anywhere else. My ID was no longer valid, my passport was out of date.

The passenger beside me asked in a friendly voice where I was from.

'Yugoslavia,' I said.

'Serb or Croat?' he asked, his face showing pride at being in the know.

At last we were recognized. For years I had watched Yugoslavs wanting to be recognized. At first we had grown up in the belief that the whole world knew about us. We needed only to cross our first frontier to be confronted with the disappointing fact that absolutely no one knew about us. That was why we nodded so joyfully when a foreigner identified us. Aha! Tito! Tito was our ID abroad. Yugoslavia — Tito. I was used to foreigners asking me what it was like behind 'the iron curtain', telling me that they had been in my *Yugoslovakia* and what a wonderful city our capital Budapest was. I was used to Swedes telling me that our migrant workers kept pigs in their bathrooms, Germans telling me about the dirty lavatories and lazy waiters on the Adriatic coast, I was used to Parisians talking about the yugo-mafia, and Londoners about 'ustashas' and 'chetniks', the fear of civilized Europe ... Ha-ha, you're a dangerous lot, down there ...

At first I got upset, started explaining, pushing the iron curtain aside, listing the republics, faiths and languages, I brought out the trump cards, the beauties of Dubrovnik, stressed the variety of cultures and landscapes in our little Balkan land, prattled on about the beauty of our coast, the advantages of our self-management system, our relative democracy, our passport which was valid everywhere, our position between West and East, our soft-communism ... And then I got tired. And in any case, how would it have been possible, now, to prove that we weren't a dangerous lot, down there? How could I have explained to anyone that the stupid phrase *'nema problema'* — which every tourist took away from Yugoslavia as a linguistic souvenir — had turned a whole country into a black farce? It was with this same conscious or unconscious thought in their minds that its crazed citizens were killing each other today ... No problem! *Nema problema!*

I looked at my neighbour, I saw that he was expecting an answer.

'I'm neither,' I said. 'I don't know who I am.'

'Oh, then you're in big trouble,' said my neighbour sympathetically.

In New York I called an American acquaintance.

'Who is it? Could you repeat your surname?' said his secretary.

I repeated my surname, spelling it.

'Ah,' said the secretary cheerfully. 'Is it with those little guys above the letters?'

Suddenly I felt slightly reconciled. I was someone with 'those little guys' above the letters of my surname.

From the Empire State Building, Yugoslavia looks like a children's toy. Brooklyn — that's Slovenia. The Brooklyn-Slovenes are diligently setting up their frontiers, their customs posts, bringing in their own money which is no longer called the 'dollar' but the 'tollar'. The Brooklyn-Slovenes are abandoning New York for ever. And there are Queens-Serbia and Bronx-Croatia. The Bronx is desperately seeking independence, insisting that it always has been independent of New York. Queens won't let it go, it seems to want to control the whole of New York. The telephone lines between the Bronx and Queens are broken, communications are blocked, the people in the Bronx watch only Bronx-TV, the people in Queens only Queens-TV. And the roads are blocked. You can only get to the Bronx via Boston, and to Queens via Chicago! The New York federal army is on the side of Queens, it's federal, it's the army, it's only natural that it should always want more territory. The Bronx is already half-destroyed, there are a lot of casualties, the inhabitants of the Bronx are ready to give their lives for their Bronx. And things are hotting up in Manhattan and bubbling in New Jersey . . . Whose side will they be on in this war which is creeping through tunnels, which is coming close to the bridges, which is knocking at their doors as well?

America watches the New York war calmly, as though it were a video-game. No one believes that the Bronx is already half-destroyed and that there are real bodies in the streets. From the Empire State Building it all looks like a children's toy. Perhaps that's why America is indifferent. Meanwhile things go on being terrible in the Bronx, people go on being killed, whole quarters are vanishing, razed to the ground.

And which is true: what you see from the top or what is happening on the streets of the Bronx? Is it true that it's all a question of perspective? From the media point of view the truth is the victory of one (truth) over others. Do the media produce the only viable truth?

In the East Village, where I was living for the time being, I found a cobbler's. In the shop were a plump little woman and the swarthy shopkeeper. There was a cassette of Russian estrade music playing. And I explained in Russian: the heels need replacing, they need sticking here.

'Where are you from?' asked the shopkeeper.

'Yugoslavia.'

'Oh,' they sighed compassionately, nodding.

'Come in an hour. I'll fix them at once,' said the shopkeeper warmly, taking my shoes.

'Good luck,' said the little woman with feeling, nodding her head. Something caught in my throat, I suddenly felt like crying, because of that momentary understanding, because of the sudden burst of brotherly warmth, because of the raw nakedness of the whole situation.

'OK, OK,' I muttered almost to myself, hurrying out of the shop.

I telephoned my mother in Zagreb.

It's just as it was when you left . . . Perhaps a bit worse. They're attacking Dubrovnik again. Vukovar has been completely demolished, they're shelling Osijek, Karlovac . . . It's all terrible. I don't know how we'll get by. They're throwing some kind of 'web' over us . . . No, don't worry, they say it isn't poisonous ... We're all right. We've just come out of the shelter ... The thing that worries me most is that you left without your winter coat. Is it cold there yet? We've got the heat on already, but not much. There's no gas, they say. Who knows how we'll manage this winter. And do they know about us over there? Do they write about us? Don't worry ... For the moment we're safe and sound.

I shatter into little pieces, I think I'll never put myself together again. It makes no difference at all whether I'm here or there, the fear is just as strong, horror wraps round me like a web. And I wonder which is reality: that before or this after? I wonder where this appalling evil erupted, this cruelty, this senseless destruction. What is this terrible need to destroy everything that was built up, to burn it, to raze it to the ground, where does it come from? What is this necessity to kill without reason or aim, just to do it, where does it come from? And which is reality: that before or this after?

When she heard that I was a writer, the young New Yorker interested in 'Eastern Europe' asked, 'So how are things now, after perestroika, I mean censorship and all that?'

'I'm sorry, but you've got the wrong country,' I said.

'Oh yes, excuse me,' she apologized. 'You're the country where there's a war on, aren't you?'

'Yes, we're the country where there's a war on.'

'I'm sorry,' she said kindly, smiling.

A grey November morning. I went out for a walk in St Mark's Place. There were a lot of homeless people asleep, pressed up against the houses; others were wriggling out of their rags and lighting their first morning cigarettes. It was still early for New York, it wasn't yet ten o'clock. The street was deserted, the trinket sellers had not yet set out their stalls.

Suddenly I felt an irresistible need to sit down here in the street for a while, to wrap myself in rags like the homeless people, to press myself against the wall of a building, to crawl into a little cardboard house.

Lit by the grey morning light, a black man was walking towards me. He stretched out his arms, waving them like wings, a black angel. For a moment his eyes met mine.

'Good morning, America!' he shouted at the top of his voice, his face contorted into a smile.

And all at once I waved my arms as well, as though I were going to take off.

'Good morning,' I said.

THE ORGANIZER

1. 'Organizer' was the first word that tripped me up and I've been stumbling over it ever since. I don't know whether it has adopted me, or I it, this word, this object, *the organizer*.

2. When I go into American supermarkets I don't look round, I walk straight ahead, to the back of the vast space crammed with things, I go to find them — organizers. There they are. The organizers glisten with a cold plastic sheen. Organizers for stockings (every stocking in its own plastic compartment), organizers for dresses, organizers for shoes, for ties, for jewellery, organizers for pullovers, folding ones with little cardboard shelves, big ones for coats. Organizers of coloured card which can be folded to make drawers, little cupboards, little wardrobes, shelves ... Special hanging organizers, so special, so collapsable, so practi-

cal, they bring order to unruly cupboards. Organizers for visiting cards (each card in its own little plastic house), organizers for pencils, for addresses and telephone numbers, for cheques and money, for manuscripts, documents, files, for every article, for every purpose, for every circumstance.

3. When I write, I number each section. That's how I organize my thoughts. Numbers seem to be the most accurate symbol of the organizer.

4. America is an organized country. Organizers permeate American everyday life like a fine-meshed net. Organizers greet the traveller as he arrives in America. At the airport passengers wait for passport control organized neatly into columns by snaking ropes. Americans arranged one behind the other (like visiting cards in an organizer) enter their own country in one organizational sequence. The *others* enter in another.

Rag snakes of organizers wind and wriggle through banks, post offices, institutions. Snakelike ropes determine the waiting person's journey from the entrance to the exit of the bank, post office, institution . . .

You can buy pizza in an organized way in America as well, if you happen to like pizza, of course. Which I do. The organizer-man shouts numbers through a microphone. I'm holding a scrap of paper I've obtained previously and I'm waiting impatiently for my turn. When I hear my number, I hurry to take my organized pizza, identified by number. It tastes better that way.

Americans aren't afraid of numbers. Except 13. That's

why the only day you can get air tickets on busy routes without much trouble is the thirteenth of the month. That's why high-rise buildings often don't have a thirteenth floor.

5. Americans walk like organizers. During lunchtime in New York, armies of organized people swarm out of their offices. Men in white shirts, suits, ties, neatly shaved and combed, women in suits, with high-heeled shoes, neat hairstyles. Many people perform the business of lunch with lunch-packs, tin cans neatly dressed in brown paper bags, sitting or standing, putting the leftovers neatly into trash cans. Only a few of them show signs of disorganization. The ones who smoke, leaning against the walls of skyscrapers. They have come down to earth from their celestial office-organizers and are blowing little smoke-rings of chaos into the air. That's how it is in Wall Street. In the Manhattan-organizer, chaos is situated between C and D Avenues, in Harlem and some other places. In the centre is order, chaos is at the edge.

6. The organizer is the only known weapon in the battle against chaos. A small innocent hanger-organizer vanquishes chaos as effectively as a dangerous machete. Because it, c-h-a-o-s, can naturally only threaten organized societies.

7. Chaos peers through a little hole in the tooth (call the dentist!), chaos creeps through neglected nails (call the pedicurist!), chaos peeps through dark curls in dyed hair

(to the hairdresser, quick!), chaos seeps through a stain on clothes (to the dry cleaners!), chaos peers through a hole in a stocking, chaos threatens from everywhere, chaos knocks on the door with the unpaid bills, with possible loss of employment, with possible serious illness, chaos hides in the little cardboard house of the homeless, chaos drips from fat passers-by, chaos grins from the faces of addicts, chaos rises in the vapour from the street sewer openings, chaos yawns from the black, burnt houses in Bronx, at night chaos rustles in the trash cans, chaos leers all around, wriggles out of dark holes, fat, terrible and black as a city rat . . .

8. That is why people invented organizers. Chaos is separated into little heaps, tidied away in shiny plastic compartments and closed with a safety zip. Zip! There. No more chaos. No more darkness.

9. I have a liking for organizers. I buy them wherever I can. My room is filling up with them. Clothes-organizers, desk-organizers . . . I haven't yet taken any action. I'm just a new arrival who buys organizers. Their cold, plastic sheen glistens. They soothe me. They are a substitute for my lost home, one day I shall tidy my own chaos away in them.

10. I don't know where my former house is, I don't know where my future house will be, I don't know whether I have a roof over my head, I don't know what to do with my childhood, what to do with my origins, with my languages, I don't know what to do with my

Croatian, my Serbian, my Slovene, or my Macedonian, I don't know what to do with my hammer and sickle, my old coat of arms and my new one, or the yellow star, what to do with the dead, with the living, I don't know what to do with the past or with the future ... I just don't know. I'm walking chaos. That's why I buy organizers.

11. In the weekly news magazine, *Vreme* (which I buy tidily in the organizer on 42nd St) I read news from my homeland. In Vukovar, having first destroyed the city and its people, the Federal Army steals 'pony-bikes'. Every soldier, every 'victor' drags a child's bicycle behind him. On their soldiers' caps is the cyrillic threat: *Silent liquidation units*. Organizers. Kill — cleanse — organize. It's terrible in Vukovar. People, soldiers, the occasional journalist. A soldier gives everyone water, a can of food and bread. 'How are you now that it's all over?' a journalist asks a woman. 'When what's over?' says the woman. 'Our house has been demolished, we've got nothing, we don't know where we're being taken, they've shelled and bombed us so much we're all out of our minds. We aren't normal people any more. What do you mean "over"?' the woman shouts furiously. The soldier offers her a can. 'Bugger off, you and your can!' says the woman. A young man turns to the soldier: 'What use is a can when you've taken our opener?'

I shut the magazine. O — opener. O — order.

38

O — organizer. Where can I tidy away my torment and my despair?

12. My shoes-organizer has 12 compartments. All my organizers have an even number of compartments. I'm aware of the importance of organization. I shall never be like my American acquaintance Judith who lives alone in a neglected house ruled by two enormous cats, while Judith dreams constantly of one day moving to Greece. No, I shall never be like the Croatian poet V who, after many years, was finally pushed out of her own flat by heaps of treacherous, disorganized rubbish. No, I shall not be like my crazy Moscow friend Zhenya who crammed his flat too full of watercolours — and in the end fell with his whole flat (oh, Soviet bungling!) and his whole watery menagerie through an entire floor. No, I don't want to be like my American friend Norman who swore that he wouldn't clean his flat until he had sorted his tax bills, and that was several months ago. I shan't be like them. They are ruined. I shall be my own office for the silent liquidation of chaos, I shall organize myself. I shall be American. I shall stop smoking. One day I shall be cold, smooth, slippery and completely plastic. Like an organizer.

MISSING

My mother collects other people's deaths, clinking them sadly like coins in a money-box.

'Did you know Petrović was dead?' asks Mother on the phone.

'Really?' I say, although I haven't a clue who Petrović is.

'Yes, imagine, he died of a heart attack,' says Mother, stressing the word heart attack.

'Oh . . .' I say.

'Poor man,' sighs Mother, ending her little verbal funeral rite. And she puts Petrović away in her imaginary money-box.

Mother tells me this sort of thing. It means she can prolong the anonymous Petrović's life for another moment, light him an invisible candle. Counting out other people's deaths like small change, she drives away her own fear.

But I'm not interested in deaths. They are so final. I'm interested in — disappearance.

About twenty years ago a Yugoslav actor disappeared. Children loved him, he acted a certain Šumenko in a children's television series. After his disappearance the newspapers were full of headlines: 'Šumenko vanishes'; 'Where has Šumenko gone?'; 'Šumenko — dead or alive?' and so on. He was never found. Either among the dead or the living.

One day my Zagreb friend Knaflec disappeared as well. People said he had gone to America. When I first went to America, someone smuggled me his phone number. I called the number, somewhere in Texas. He answered, but he wasn't my friend Knaflec any more. Now it doesn't occur to me to call him. Because he has — vanished.

And then a journalist took up my favourite theme of disappearance and wrote an article about it. It turned out that 2,847 people had disappeared in Yugoslavia that year. I can even remember the figure. That year 2,847 Yugoslavs could not be found among either the living or the dead.

New York confuses me most.

As I walk through the streets of New York I often think I must be having a nightmare. I see a man with a plastic bag. There's a long stick of American celery poking out of it. And I see clearly: it's my friend Nenad. Hey, Nenad, I shout. Hey, what are you doing here? He looks at me but doesn't recognize me. Goodness, I whisper, confused. He shrugs his shoulders and walks on carrying his long stick of celery in his bag.

A taxi passes. My friend Berti's in it. Hey, Berti! The taxi stops at a crossing, the light's red. Hey, Berti! Berti looks at me through the window, he smiles, but he doesn't recognize me. What's this, I think, if he were here, if that were Berti, he'd surely say hello, I think ... But I'm not entirely sure ...

In the park I watch a cleaner sweeping up dry leaves. He blows the leaves away with an enormous vacuum cleaner, making rustling golden yellow heaps. A magician. For a moment I clearly see the profile of my friend Pavle. Hey, Pavle, what are you doing here? I shout. Hey! ... I go up to him and tap him on the shoulder. He turns round and says, in English, with no foreign accent: 'Stop that, Madam, or I'll call the police.'

And I stop. The newspaper seller on the corner is my Zagreb acquaintance Vilma. I buy papers from her every day, on the corner of Eighth and University Streets. I gaze at her for a long time, put the money into her hand significantly and take my *New York Times*. I don't say anything, I don't insist any more, I pretend I don't know she is Vilma. Thank you, have a nice day.

Here in Middletown it's quite different. It's a small place, I don't know anyone, I'm a stranger, they are at home. But still, I remember every face, to be on the safe side. The assistant at Bob's, the cashier at Waldbaum's, the waiter at the Opera House, the policeman by the Clock Tower. I let my glance range over the names in the local telephone directory. Brigith, Gloria; Kilby, Peter;

Hills, Karen ... I don't know anyone. I feel safe and calm. Everything is as it should be. I'm a stranger, they are local, at home.

At about 12 o'clock each day the postman comes. I open the Zagreb papers of 29 November 1991. I read an article about missing persons. 30,000 missing persons have been registered in Croatia, writes the author. People are looking for vanished brothers, husbands, wives, children, parents. Not only have several villages and towns disappeared, but these 30,000 people as well. They can no longer be found among either the living or the dead.

Terrible, I think. It's just as well I'm here, where it's safe. I'm a stranger here, they're all at home, everything is as it should be. Someone called Peter lives near me, someone called Gloria, someone called Karen. I'm protected, nothing can happen to me.

Suddenly I hear a bell, I go to the door, open it — and unknown people spill into my flat. They pour in uncontrollably, like a flood, women, children, old men, wounded people, soldiers. I'm Željko, a young man introduces himself, it's two months since I disappeared somewhere near Pirot, my sister Ljubica Oreški is looking for me ... I'm a mother, murmurs a woman, I disappeared in September, somewhere near Drniš; my son, Rade Brakus, is looking for me.

And I understand, here they are, all 30,000. Come in, I say, find places to sit, make yourselves comfortable, we'll manage somehow. They arrange themselves quietly. There are so many of them, I think, and they all fit into my small flat, as though they were transparent, I think, as though they were cards, one fits over the other. That's because they've disappeared, I think, that's why they're so — collapsable.

And as I cook a meal to feed them all, I think about the fact that the globe is like an egg-timer, like two joined vessels, there's a copy of everything, as in a library. There's a Berlin here in my neighbourhood, ten minutes' drive from here, West and East, nothing has been left out. There's a copy of everything somewhere, especially here, there's Paris in Texas, and Moscow and Madrid and Copenhagen and Venice and London and Hamburg, and New York is only New Amsterdam... The missing don't disappear, then, they simply spring up somewhere else, in some other place, in my flat, for instance. It's all right, I think, everything's all right, there's no need to worry, I'll look for your brother, Ljubica Oreški...

The telephone rings, it's my mother from Zagreb.

'Did you know...' my mother begins slowly and I already anticipate the familiar, soft clinking in the receiver.

'I know, mother, there's no need to tell me. They're here... We're all here...' I say, and I hear a rich clinking like a slot-machine suddenly spitting out a whole heap of coins.

MANUAL

'I'm madly in love ... But, it's Madeline ... he doesn't want me,' my American friend Norman complains. Speaking Croatian, Norman uses the feminine gender when he talks about himself, and masculine for the tender, green-eyed Madeline, who 'doesn't want' him.

'Oh?' I say.

'I shall go to Croatia to die,' says this infatuated doctor of political science who once spent a year in Zagreb on a Fulbright scholarship.

'What would you do there, it's not your homeland.'

'I'd thought of killing myself in any case because of Madeline. It would be better to die in a romantic way.'

'If you have to kill yourself, it would be better to do it in a — practical way,' I say, adding: 'There's a handbook for that sort of thing.'

'There's a manual?' he asks, in a brighter tone.

Manuals are the American bible. American everyday life is a culture of manuals.

Sacred handbooks or instructions, they are like the innocent little scrap of material with a mass of words that you find attached to a small plush teddy bear, a child's toy. Everything is written on that scrap: the material the bear's made of, and what you have to do with it, not in the mouth, not near the fire, not this and not that ... With instructions for use a little plush bear becomes a serious matter.

Americans shop as though they were taking an important exam. Buying ordinary tennis shoes can take an hour. Americans establish a kind of oral manual with the shop assistant. What are the laces made of, can you easily move your toes, what about the tongue, and the sole, and how flexible are they, and what are they made of, and what's the lining like, and what's the difference between these and those ... The assistant gives instructions as though he were an orthopaedic surgeon rather than a shop assistant. The American purchaser listens and talks as though he were a patient rather than an ordinary customer.

At the entrance of vast American supermarkets, the buyer is met by various types of free propaganda material. Enough for a whole newspaper stand. Just buying bread, a person can learn something about radon — radioactive gas — the new bogeyman of American daily life; as he buys cornflakes he can learn something about panic disorder, about symptoms which until a moment before he had romantically believed were a sign of sudden anxiety or metaphysical dread (I always used to go for the latter, myself), and now, it turns out that it's ordinary, insurmountable fear. As he buys his thanksgiving turkey, a person can inform himself about how to reduce his income tax; as he buys mineral water, he can obtain free information about bedwetting, which (bedwetting that is) can cause serious problems in later life: it may threaten the self-image, or ruin one's self-esteem. As he buys sausages, a person can learn how to become rich or how to buy a house; as he selects a boneless joint, he can take a free booklet, *The Dating Page*, and discover how to find a suitable partner for a life à deux.

And while I, a foreigner, am overcome by panic disorder because I don't know what to do with the booklet full of coupons (guaranteeing me *big savings*, — that is I can't decide whether I want a boneless joint for only $3.59 or a companion, male, healthy, handsome, a non-smoker, who enjoys dancing, skiing, sailing, parachuting and romantic candle-lit dinners; that is I don't know whether I should get rich first so that I can buy the joint for only $3.59, or whether to buy the joint and then find a partner for life — meanwhile the ordinary American swims through it all like a fish through water. He is used to a system which leads him to his desired aim, like a video-game.

But in order to reach that aim, you have to master the instructions. Intuition is a completely useless faculty here, besides, it's something possessed by the chosen, and the equitable American system offers you what is

47

available to everyone. Manuals, instructions, handbooks. You have to read, to read carefully, to read right through, without skipping. Besides, it is precisely in the places where the reader's attention begins to flag that you find large letters proclaiming KEEP READING! So, you have to keep on reading, not interrupting, not missing anything out (DON'T MISS THIS!). There is nothing in this world that can't be mastered with the aid of clear instructions.

The culture of manuals which lead you to your desired aim is effective because it is based on a deeply mythical assumption. Every manual is based on the archetype of the labyrinth, it is a future and former fairy-tale about Ivan the Fool who reaches his desired aim by mastering all the obstacles, following strict instructions (strict!). And his aim, of course, is a kingdom and a beautiful queen! Those who sin, dissidents with respect to the system, those who, like Pandora, open the box despite instructions to the contrary, such people mean trouble both for themselves and for the world. The video-game is in this sense a modern fairy-tale: the culture of the manual has its hero, its video-game player, its Ivan the Fool. Whoever follows the instructions, must reach the desired aim. No one can shake an American's fundamental belief in that truth. *Keep reading! Keep living!*

'And what if he doesn't? What if he doesn't reach the desired aim, despite the instructions?' asks my sceptical, my suspicious, my cynical, my lazy, my ironic, my destructive brain. And what if he doesn't?

And I can see myself already, I know, I give up at

the very beginning: I'll never be rich, I'll never have a beautiful house and a life partner keen on sailing, skiing, flying, a non-smoker what's more, I'll never get a tax rebate, I'll never lose all my superfluous pounds, I'll never get my body into a satisfactory shape, I'll never buy a boneless joint for only $3.59, I'll never stop smoking, I'll never win the lottery, I shan't, I shan't ever . . .

And that's only right. I'm not master of myself, I'm not master of anything. When I investigate all the depths of my dissidence, when I reach the very last 'I shan't' or 'I can't' (which is the same thing here), there's still a chance for me! America has taken that into account. *Final exit*. The manual. A handbook for suicide, or more refinedly — for self-deliverance. I'll read the final instructions carefully, slowly, there's no rush. I'll choose my final exit like a gourmet dish in the best restaurant. I'll run my eyes slowly over the menu: *Death Hollywood-Style, Bizarre Ways to Die, Self-Deliverance via the Plastic Bag* . . . I'll buy myself a little calculator so that I can convert ounces to grammes, I'll learn everything, I'll study everything, I'll be a perfectionist.

Besides, in the world of manuals everything is easy, painless and safe. Nevertheless I trust in Unpredictability, as the Great Poetic Idea. Because perhaps on the screen of the new interactive computer, in those new manuals, where you use your finger instead of the computer mouse, where an ordinary finger has the power of a magic wand — perhaps, by touching a little astral circle on the computer, I'll be able to open a pass, a door, perhaps like Alice I shall slip through a tunnel into another world, the world on the other side of the Manual.

The phone rings, it's my American friend Norman.

'Madeline loves me, he told me today,' he says cheerfully.

'Oh?' I say.

'It was silly of me to say I'd kill myself. Madeline wants me. Did you hear?'

'I heard.'

'So why are you sad?'

'Dubrovnik has been bombed.'

'Oh? I'm sorry, I'm really sorry,' he says, genuinely upset. We say nothing for a while, and then my American friend asks cautiously, 'What do you think, did Madeline really mean it when he said he loved me?'

SHRINK

For some time now I've had a shrink. No American with an iota of self-respect knows who he or she is: that's why every American has a shrink. And, although I'm a foreigner, I do have self-respect and I don't know who I am. My shrink is a woman, a bleached blonde very like the star of my childhood, Doris Day.

'You see, there was a bad earthquake in Montenegro a few years ago. Afterwards a journalist asked a peasant what it had been like. Well, said the peasant, I was in my house when I felt something shake. I went outside and I saw it: the epicentre! I ran to the left, but the epicentre followed me, I ran to the right, and the epicentre followed me again.'

'How amusing,' says my shrink with a faint smile.

'It's not amusing,' I say. 'That's why I've come to you. You see, the epicentre has followed me. What can I tell you ... The ground is trembling under my feet, I keep seeing double, everything seems so fragile it'll shatter at any minute,' I say like an intelligent person who expresses herself in metaphors and can't be bothered with details.

'Please don't express yourself in metaphors, be concrete. To begin with, just tell me what Montenegro is,' says my shrink emphatically.

And I explain, why not. In the general disorder it's absolutely immaterial where I start from. I list them all: Montenegro and Slovenia, Croatia, Bosnia and Hercegovina, Macedonia and Serbia. I mention the two former autonomous provinces as well, Vojvodina and Kosovo.

'Why former?' asks the shrink.

I explain that too. And I enumerate them all: Slovenes and Croats, Serbs and Muslims, Montenegrins and Albanians, Jews and Italians, Gypsies and Romanians, Bulgarians and Rusyns, Hungarians and Czechs . . . I enumerate them all, I don't leave anything out.

'Keep it brief, please, so that we can get to the fundamental source of your frustration as quickly as possible,' says my shrink.

'I started from the epicentre but you asked me to explain what Montenegro was,' I say indignantly.

'All right, all right,' mumbles my shrink. 'Go on.'

And I go on, I explain the history of Yugoslavia, I explain my own personal history along the way, I drag my grandmothers and grandfathers out of the dust, not for my sake, but I think, maybe she, the shrink, needs to know, I recall my own childhood, I leave nothing out, not my pioneer scarf, nor the work camp, nor Tito's baton . . .

'Wait. What was Tito's baton?'

And I explain. A piece of wood or metal, a hand-made hollow stick, and for years some 22 million Yugoslavs stuffed little scraps of paper into the hollow — greetings for Tito's birthday, symbolically passing the stick from hand to hand like a pledge of brotherhood and unity.

'I don't quite see, but it's obviously a phallic symbol,' says my shrink professionally.

'Of course,' I say. 'I come from a phallic culture, male; a culture of batons, sticks and knives, according to need. But let's leave that for now, that wouldn't get us anywhere.'

'But that's obviously what's brought you . . . where you are now,' she observes acidly.

'But you sucked on Coca-Cola and waved those "pom-poms" about when you were a cheerleader in school and you're normal,' I say impudently.

'You're right. I'd almost forgotten,' my Doris Day murmurs nostalgically. 'Carry on.'

And I carry on. I leave nothing out. I talk about socialism, about our mentality, collectivism, about the collective *we*, instead of the individual *I*, about the *we* who is never responsible, in the name of whom a bright future was always promised us, in the name of whom people are slaughtering each other now . . .

'I see. If you had a developed culture of the "self" everything would be far better for your — '

'Then we'd have individual and not collective madness.'

'Explain.'

And I explain. I give her a short history of dishonour. I talk about mythic, tribal thinking, about primitive, savage ways, about illiteracy, about the criminal mentality, about theft, lies, the legitimation of lies, the culture of lies, obstinacy, about the newly composed rural mentality which weeps as it kills and kills as it weeps . . .

'Explain more concretely. I don't understand anything you're saying.'

And I explain. I enumerate dates, names, I give the results of democratic elections in percentages, I list the parties in power and those in opposition, I list the names of leaders, events, cities . . .

'Milosevik . . . Vu-ko-var.' The shrink struggles with the names.

And I go on. I talk about the savagery of the army, about Serbian and Montenegrin volunteers plundering Dubrovnik, about collective paranoia, about lies, about the destruction of Croatian towns, about murdered children, about burnt villages, about massacres, about refugees, about drunkenness, about madness, about the cult of the knife . . .

And I notice that my shrink's hands are trembling slightly, she pretends to write a diagnosis on a piece of paper.

'That's enough of that. You seem to be recounting horror films. I doubt that any of that can be taking place in the heart of Europe, on the threshold of the twenty-first century,' says my shrink in a school teacher's voice. 'Now tell me the problem,' she continues sternly.

'My problem is the fact that it is all true, and not a horror film.'

'Tell me about your personal problem,' she says, stressing *personal*, as though all the above does not belong in the register of personal problems.

And I gladly go on explaining. I am a divided personality, I see everything in double exposures, I am a house inhabited by parallel worlds, everything exists simultaneously in my head. I look at the American flag and suddenly I seem to see little red sickles and hammers instead of white stars. I look at a television advertisement for necklaces, that's the kind I find most soothing, and instead of pearl necklaces for only 65 dollars — I see a slit throat. I walk down Fifth Avenue and suddenly see the buildings falling like card houses . . . Everything is mixed up in my head, everything exists simultaneously, nothing has just one meaning any more, nothing is firm any longer, not the earth, not frontiers, not people, not houses . . . Everything is so fragile it seems it will shatter any minute . . .

'And the most terrible thing of all', I say in a tormented voice, 'is that I think it's my fault, that I'm carrying the virus . . . At the moment I'm most anxious about the Empire State Building and Brooklyn Bridge . . .'

'Nothing can happen to you. You're quite safe here,' says my shrink with conviction.

'I was quite safe there too but it happened.'

'You're simply in a state of shock, everything'll be all right.'

'But what about the virus? What if at this moment, while the two of us are talking, the Empire State Building is collapsing! And you tell me that everything'll be all right!'

'You know yourself that it's impossible!'

'That's what I thought about Dubrovnik!'

'Jesus Christ, that's really too much! Work on your self-esteem, which has been seriously damaged. I'll see you on Friday week,' says my Doris Day resolutely bringing the session to an end. Her hands are trembling slightly, and she looks paler than she did at the beginning.

And I take her advice. I do yoga every day, I work at myself, my *self*, I am the centre of the world, nothing else interests me, nothing else exists, and no one can distract me from my path. I look at my outstretched leg like an object worthy of respect, I don't think about anything, I listen to music, the best, stress busters, new age, and I've ordered a brain supercharger, I'm expecting it to arrive any day now ... I've quite forgotten about my shrink, as though I'd never even been there ...

The telephone rings. I don't pick up the receiver. I'm used to that too. I sit in the lotus-pose, I don't stir. I'm beginning to see the results of my work on myself. It doesn't occur to me to move and answer the call. A familiar voice pours out of the answering machine.

'Hello? What's the matter with you? Hello? Where are

you? Why don't you answer? Please, call me. I need your help. It's here, in my clinic. The epicentre! I don't know what to do. Everything is shaking, I'm seeing double exposures, everything seems so fragile it'll shatter at any minute . . .'

JOGGING

'It's terrible. Madeline's left me again. He's gone off with someone else. I can't go on like this. I've had it,' Norman complains in Croatian. His despair runs along the telephone wires, dripping into my sensitive ear like warm wax, softening the sharp edge of the wrongly used genders.

'Everything'll be all right,' I say consolingly.

'No, it won't,' is all he says.

'Cheer up!' I say, realizing at once that I've said something wrong. You should never utter words of consolation in a language that isn't your own.

'Tell me what's happening to me, for God's sake,' says my friend in a voice which sends uncomfortable shivers down my spine, mine, an expert on Russian literature!

'It's all as simple as ABC, Norman,' I say. 'You're head-over-heels in love. And your Madeline is only making it worse, with her strategy of "now yes, now no".'

'No,' sighs Norman decisively into the receiver. 'It's not so simple, it's all much more complicated . . .' and after a long pause he adds in a bleak voice, 'Perhaps the reason I feel so bad is that I haven't been jogging for a whole week.'

I have white plastic blinds on the windows of my flat. In the morning, as soon as I get out of bed, I go straight to the window. I part the blind a little, let a horizontal shaft of light into the room and lean my forehead against the cold plastic. Secretly I peer through the horizontal gaps. I wait. Looking at the empty stadium like this makes my warm drowsiness last longer. And there he is, he's coming, my solitary jogger. His red hair tied in a pony-tail, marble-white face, invisible eyes, he runs rhythmically and easily. I can see it's cold outside by the breath coming from his mouth. One-two, one-two, my lonely runner runs, my jo-gg-er, my morning light, my sweet voyeuristic sin, jo-gg-errrr . . . Jo-gg-errr: the tip of my tongue slips along my palate, and then suddenly turns up like a little snake and slides back down my throat.

The runner goes out of sight, I can't see him any more, but I know: he'll come this way again tomorrow. 'Jogger!' I toss the gutteral sound out of my mouth. In the quiet emptiness of my room the word tinkles softly like a little Chinese rattle made of mother-of-pearl.

The weather in Connecticut is deceptive. The strong winter sun makes the geometrically straight lines of the town even sharper, even straighter. Light and shadow follow each other regularly like a chessboard. The figures on the board are called: *Waldbaum, Caldor, Sears, Stop Shop* . . . On sunny days like this a cold wind whips your face unexpectedly, darting out of ambush and sweeping into the next road. In Main Street is the Clock Tower with an enormous clock at the top. A policeman walks under the tower. The hands on the clock are long, black and sharp like the shadow of the policeman's baton. The clock and the policeman harmonize the rhythm of the day.

At night I often wake up disturbed by the ticking of an inner clock. I get up, go to the window, slowly part the blinds and stare into the darkness. I often feel that he is here, my jogger. He stops, looks at me with his head on one side like some slender-legged animal and waits. In the dark I imagine his thighs dewy with sweat, I feel his regular pulse, I feel the warmth of his breath. Wrapped in emptiness like a blanket I stare into the darkness, for a long time.

Every day I buy something. I buy secretly. In the shop I pretend I'm buying things for my brother, my husband, my friend, it's just what I need for my nephew, I say, those headbands, you know, that sportsmen wear . . . Aha, a *sweat band* says the patient assistant and brings me the bands I want. I learn the words, I buy things in order to learn the words, I learn the words in order to buy the things. *Jog-a-lites* are little yellow markers, ribbons, circles, for runners who run in the dark.

Every day I buy something and bring it to my flat. I

lay the things out in my room as a bride would her wedding dress, I look at them, touch them, but I still don't dare wear any of them. I don't tell anyone about my passion, I shop in secret, I drag the booty to my lair.

One-two, one-two, runs my lonely runner. I make out his thighs dewy with sweat, little drops of sweat on his upper lip. The deceptive Connecticut wind whips his pale face. One-two, one-two, runs my lonely runner. *The ivory framework of the limbs so light moved like a pair of balances deflected, there glided through the coat a gleam of white, and on the forehead, where the beams collected, stood, like a moon-lit tower, the horn so bright, at every footstep proudly re-erected. Its mouth was slightly open, and a trace of white through the soft down of grey and rose (whitest of whites) came from the gleaming teeth; its nostrils panted gently for repose. Its gaze, though, checked by nothing here beneath, projecting pictures into space, brought a blue saga-cycle to a close.**

Running shoes: $78.99; sweat suit: $73.29; sweat socks: $5.99; sweat shirt: $12.99; sweat pants: $19.00; sweat band: $5.99; T-shirt: $10.50.

At night I often wake up disturbed by the ticking of an inner clock. I get up, go to the window, slowly part the blinds and let horizontal shafts of moonlight fall into the room. For a long time I stare into the darkness. And

*Rainer Maria Rilke, 'The Unicorn', translated by J.B. Leishman.

then without switching on the light I put on my new, clean T-shirt, I put on my snow-white cotton socks, my new warm cotton tracksuit, over that I put a light nylon windcheater, then I take my new white running shoes, try them carefully, like a samurai testing the blade of his sword. On my head, like a wedding garland, I place a brightly coloured sweat band.

I go to the window, stare into the darkness and wait patiently. First I see two bright yellow fluorescent spots in the dark. Two yellow spots chase each other in the night and then disappear.

He is standing outside my window, he is standing illuminated by the moonlight, looking at me with his head on one side, waiting ... I go outside, the deceptive Connecticut wind whips my face. I go up to him, I touch his red hair with my hand, run it over his face. My jogger, I whisper, my sweet voyeuristic sin ... He holds out his hand to me without speaking, draws me after him and we start to run in the darkness. One-two, one-two ... Suddenly I feel that we are weightless, we are rising to the sky, we follow the paths marked out by the street-lights. In the darkness isolated letters shine like huge stars: *Waldbaum, Caldor, Stop Shop, Sears* ... One-two, one-two, we run lightly, silently, as though on cotton-wool ... The clock on the Clock Tower is round and bright as a moon. We run above Main Street, turn into Court Street, we run above High Street ... One-two, one-two, my jogger, rhythm of my breathing, jogger, rhythm of my heart, jogger, fire of my loins, jogger,

jogger, jogger ... *Keep on repeating this word to the end of the page, typesetter ...*

'She brought me a mouse,' says Beka, pointing in my direction.

'How could I have "brought" it?' I protest.

'The mouse appeared when you did.'

'Perhaps it was here before but you didn't notice it,' says the actress soothingly.

'I'd certainly have noticed it, if it was,' says Beka.

'How did it get into the flat?' asks the director.

'Through the ventilation grille, they get in through the ventilation grilles out here,' says the archaeologist.

'In any case, there weren't ever any mice in this flat before,' says Beka, shaking her head.

'New York is full of mice, it's perfectly natural that one should turn up in your flat,' says the journalist.

'All large cities are full of mice. Amsterdam, for instance, one day it'll be overrun with mice.'

'And Paris.'

'And Berlin.'

'I don't give a damn about Berlin! Everything was all right in my flat until she appeared,' says Beka, pointing in my direction.

We are sitting in Beka's flat, the lights of New York are twinkling through the window, we are chattering, nattering, shifting the words around our mouths like nuts, taking care not to bite into the kernel.

We are all here 'by chance'. Some of us are teaching at American universities for a semester or two, some have scholarships, some are passing through as tourists. An actress, an old film director, a young film director, a psychologist, a journalist, a writer, an archaeologist. All from more or less the same branch of activity, all more or less the same age (forty or so), all out of more or less the same social, intellectual and ideological kindergarten.

We look at each other, we feel uneasy and sympathetic at the same time, as with members of our own family. Because once (oh, so long ago) we all wore a pioneer scarf round our necks, we all waved flags to greet visitors with unpronounceable names (nkrumah, sirimavobandaranaike, haileselassie), we all learned our letters from the same ABC (H — for homeland), and sentences from the same First Reading Book ('Cherish brotherhood and unity, your most precious gift,' Tito) . . . Oh, when was that! And can it really have been our own, shared history or just a film in which we took part as child extras? And then we grew up and forgot it all. And then

65

we all scattered through our own lives. We popped over to Trieste, to London, to Paris, to New York for a while, but it didn't occur to anyone really to go anywhere, why should we, why should any of us really go anywhere, life was good — skiing in winter, in the Slovene mountains, summer at the sea, the Adriatic.

No, no one did go anywhere. Nothing, actually, ever happened.

For a moment in Beka's flat we stopped, for a moment we all wondered to ourselves how it was that we weren't all chattering in some Zagreb, Sarajevo or Belgrade café, but were here, in New York, and how it was that there were suddenly so many of us, and we all knew each other, what a coincidence, and how was it that we were all, more or less, the same age ...

No, no one had gone anywhere. And nothing actually ever happened. Except perhaps to the actress. She had been declared a traitor. By both sides. West and East. Actress-traitor! Actress-traitor!

Don't take it personally, we say to the actress. Some have died, others have fled, some have lost the roof over their heads, others their career, some are dead, others still alive, no one is the same any more.

No, no one had gone anywhere. And nothing actually ever happened. Except perhaps to the director. Once, twenty years earlier, he had made a film. And he was put in prison. He came out of prison and left the country. Then went back. Now he has left again. He cannot bear to go through the same thing all over again.

I'm fifty already, says the old director.

Don't take it personally, we say to the old director. Some have died, others have fled, some have lost the roof over their heads, others their career, some are dead, others still alive, no one is the same any more.

I'll get a job as a waiter, says the young director. How could I direct anything here? There are thousands like me. I feel like a penguin at the North Pole.

South Pole, says Beka.

Why?

Because penguins live at the South Pole.

And I'll sell garbage from the communist store-room, says the journalist. I'll give them the expected picture of the world, stereotypes of life behind 'the iron curtain', stereotypes about grey, alienated Eastern Europe standing in line for sour cabbage.

But we never stood in line for sour cabbage, we observe.

So what, it's important to maintain the general stereotype and sell it. I'll sell our yugo-souvenirs as well, our Balkan myth, our sickle, hammer and knife. Tomorrow it'll be too late, tomorrow the whole world will have forgotten it all in any case, insists the journalist.

I simply can't go back. It all makes me sick, says the actress.

No, no one had gone anywhere . . .

Except that we may have arrived too late. The last fragment of the Berlin Wall has been sold. Lenin's cap and Stalin's moustache have been sold, says the psychologist, shaking his head.

What are you on about, what are Lenin's cap and Stalin's moustache to us? asks Beka.

I'll get a job as a waiter. What else can I do? Show my films around American universities for a hundred dollars a time? There's a recession here too. We came at the wrong time.

No, no one had gone anywhere. And nothing actually ever happened.

Whenever it was, it would have been the wrong time, says the writer. We're unnecessary, over there and over here.

We didn't reconstruct ourselves at the right time, we're has-beens. Now there are new actresses, new directors, new journalists, new writers in the homeland, says the psychologist.

Which homeland? asks Beka seriously.

It all happened too fast, because I refused to participate, and I refused because I was disgusted, because I was afraid ... what's the difference. No one's going to ask the reason any more, says the old director.

I feel just like the Russian émigrés in Paris or Berlin seventy years ago, says the psychologist.

They've destroyed everything I'd been digging up for twenty years, says the archaeologist. Twenty years! Layer after layer, piece by piece, for twenty years. Now it's all back underground again.

I simply can't go on. I haven't changed out of my pyjamas for ages now. I spend the whole time feeling sleepy. All I want to do is sleep, says the actress.

Don't take it personally. Some have died, others have

fled, others have lost the roof over their heads, others their career, some are dead, others still alive, some have lost their homeland, others have acquired one, the only thing that is true is that no one is the same any more, says the writer.

I don't want to stay, I don't want to go back, what can I do? asks the director.

And do you realize that we are all roughly the same age as Yugoland, the one the cat ate? The mouse the cat ate, says the journalist.

'Hey, do you want to see it?' asks Beka holding up the definitively dead mouse in an efficient American mousetrap.

'Isn't it small!' says the actress, touched.

'Come and throw it into the trash with me,' says Beka.

And we follow Beka obediently into the corridor, to the trash shoot. Beka opens the little door and throws the mousetrap into the hole. The sound is long and loud, completely out of proportion to the object that provoked it.

'There,' says Beka, shutting the little door decisively.

And we follow her back into the flat. The New York lights twinkle lavishly in the windows. New York twinkles like a mouse, like thousands of tiny mice, like thousands of Mickey Mice.

ADDICT

America is a little bit like a hairdresser's salon. All hairdressers' salons all over the world are the same. And that's because they aren't actually salons but a model of human behaviour. When I say America has something 'hairdressery' about it, that's the model I'm thinking of.

As soon as I appear at the door of a hairdresser's salon, I am drawn into its focus — the eye of the Maestro. The Maestro might at that moment be behind a partition mixing dyes, he might have his back to me, he might be snapping his scissors over someone's head, but his gaze, cast like a terrible hook, transforms me into what in fact I am: a being in need of a haircut.

There are all sorts of Maestros: friendly, curt, talkative, silent, all sorts of different types, but the relationship between the Maestro and the customer is always the same — that of master and victim.

It's foolish to expect anything else since your head,

one way or another, is always in his hands. Whether he will follow my instructions, whether he will make of my head what I want or what he wants, whether I shall ever be seen again in his salon, whether I shall give him a tip, is entirely irrelevant. He, the Maestro, is naturally in charge of the situation.

And when he has finished serving me (or creating me, whichever), he always asks the same question:

'Are you pleased?'

A question, in other words, which never expects a negative answer, in any salon in the world. Because as a general rule it never gets one. That is one of the rules of the genre.

'Yes,' I hiss through clenched teeth, although, of course, I'm not. That is one of the rules of the genre as well. My genre. Because I never go to the hairdresser in order to be pleased, but so as to be displeased.

However, what makes my displeasure greater than the usual, expected displeasure of the genre, is his, the Maestro's, unshakeable conviction that I *must* be pleased. And how could I not be? I came in with greasy, neglected hair (*before*) and look at me now (*after*)! My hair is so shiny and neatly cut!

The Maestro's question — are you pleased? — is exactly the same as the question I am often asked by Americans:

'You'll be staying here, won't you?'

One of my American nightmares is going into a shop.

71

As soon as I enter I'm met by the assistant's smiling face.

'How are you today?'

'Fine,' I hiss between clenched teeth, then I blush and examine the tips of my shoes.

'How are you doing?'

'Fine,' I repeat more loudly, take a breath and look at the assistant.

She, poor thing, has no idea that she's dead. How many of them have I already liquidated with a glance! Simply because they oblige me to pronounce the innocent little word: fine.

Once, a colleague of mine — one of those who pronounce the words Foucault, Derrida, Lacan and Baudrillard with the same familiarity as the words mum, dad and granny — took me to a restaurant. It was in Los Angeles.

'There are only four restaurants like this in the whole of America right now,' he said as we made our way to the restaurant. 'Now at last you'll understand what postmodernism really is,' he added, with the kind of enthusiasm he might have used for, say, lobster in orange sauce.

The restaurant was large and noisy. And it really did resemble a postmodernist classroom crammed with objects of visual instruction. It was a museum of Americana and everything was there: real and fake quotes from American films and television series, from American history (which we know, of course, from American films and television series), from American everyday life, American painting (pictures which reflected that everyday life hyperrealistically). Everything was there: quote by quote, quote on quote; everything was mixed up with everything else in a kind of vast American salad. American everyday life was formulated a long time ago, and it produced the American myth, then the American myth — the stereotype — produced American everyday life, and everyday life — perpetuating that same stereotype — permanently produced that same myth, just as it was there, in that restaurant, transforming it into a life-myth show ... Or something like that ...

The menu offered naked quotations as well: we obediently ordered hamburgers and Coke. Waiters dressed as clowns entertained the customers zealously. They might lie on your table holding the plate and grin into your face while they spun the plate over their head as though they were about to spill the contents into your lap. Clown-photographers strutted about, taking pictures of customers with cheap polaroid cameras, and then obliging them to buy the proof of their own enjoyment. One group of merrymakers had ordered a huge cake; they were throwing cream at each other, enjoying themselves like the actors in old comic films.

There was general uproar in the restaurant. It was an aggressive synopsis of American happiness, that image of happiness the American media — films, series, advertisements — had been producing for years; an image of happiness which life itself now zealously imitated. The model proved its efficacity for the thousandth time: people were enjoying themselves.

A stout woman, a camp-commandant in a clown's costume, some kind of supervisor, was carefully surveying the level of happiness in the restaurant. At one moment she caught my eye. Like an accurate camera the Ring Mistress recorded my inner dissatisfaction. She immediately pointed at me and summoned the whole room to do the same.

'There, in the corner, there's a face that's not smiling. Yes, take a good look, that woman there, in the black dress,' she shrieked into the microphone.

Then, grinning at me, she playfully wagged her finger. The whole room did the same, enjoying the collective repetition of the gesture. The orchestra struck up 'Don't worry, be happy' (what else) and they soon forgot about me. I tugged my postmodernist colleague by the sleeve and we went out. My indoctrinated European brain started to run the familiar images of totalitarian happiness, images of parades, happy masses acting as a collective body . . .

'America has imposed the dictatorship of happiness,' I mumbled in a feeble voice.

'It's only a restaurant you can enter and leave whenever you feel like it,' said my colleague, bristling slightly. At that moment he was defending American democracy more than he was soothing my sudden dread. And, of course, he was right. It was only a restaurant. And, besides, only one of four similar ones in the whole of America.

'You'll be staying here, won't you?' Americans often ask

me. The tone of the question never implies the possibility of a negative reply. And what else could I say? And my hair is shiny and neatly cut, after all!

My Zagreb acquaintance Ranko M. is a confirmed misery. Whenever we meet, he lets fly lengthy verbal monologues. Against the state, past, present and future; against politicians, home-grown and foreign; against his mother who ruined him, although his father was no better; against the legal system, against small children, although bigger ones are no better; against dogs and cats, although he finds parrots, as house pets, equally obnoxious; against Croats, against Serbs, but also against the French, who are insupportable, as are the English, Germans and the Americans, God knows; against the sun that shines, against the rain that falls, against the globe that turns in the wrong direction, against the universe that is governed by total chaos . . . Nothing you can do will cheer up my Zagreb colleague Ranko M., nothing will console him, that's how he is, a confirmed misery.

Once he called on me, but this time he misjudged his strength, he didn't measure out his hatred accurately, and, after letting off his verbal rifle fire in all directions, he came to an abrupt end, like a New Year firecracker. His head suddenly fell onto the table and my acquaintance Ranko M. simply stopped. I froze. A stroke, I thought, and then I heard a reassuring, steady snoring. I watched this sleeping spasm on my table, listened to his contented snoring, and thought how varied misery is, full of fine, rich nuances.

Even intellectuals succumb to the American dictatorship of happiness. The great American writer William Styron wrote a national bestseller entitled *Darkness Visible*. This personal little book of 84 personal pages is the confession of a temporary dissident from the régime of happiness, who returns repentant to the régime and records his terrible dissident experiences. With absolute seriousness — which is a quite normal form of everyday behaviour in American culture, while in other less serious cultures it would be only the hysterical seriousness of a hypochondriac — William Styron describes his medical history. He does not forget the date of his first attack of depression (October 1985, in Paris), nor does he forget that on that occasion he had left a cheque for $25,000 in a restaurant (the cheque was soon found, luckily). With tedious precision (or simply the precision demanded by the genre of the medical history) the bestselling writer reveals to his extensive reading public which pills he took and which doctors he consulted. In the great writer's bestseller there is not a word about his feelings, they are all lumped under 'inexplicable agony', his depression is 'a simulacrum of all the evil of the world'; and 'a dark wood' or 'an abyss' from which the writer emerged personally in order to prove to America that depression is 'conquerable'.

To be depressive is the worst thing that can happen, it's a kind of socially unacceptable, undesirable emptiness, which can be transformed with the correct choice of pills and doctors into socially acceptable, desirable emptiness. And that is of course being 'fine', being happy.

The American publishing industry is simply an image of the American system of values, and for five hundred years it has been doing nothing other than build the myth of the 'pioneer'. Americans love 'pioneers', their own mythical identity-kit, and so books by all kinds of 'victors' will be in the bestseller list: books by people who have overcome serious illness, ugliness, superfluous pounds, the suffering caused by rape and other, less extreme social tribulations, by people who have climbed something, swum or sailed something, walked, run or driven somewhere . . .

Another big national bestseller, which was also a 'pioneering' personal story, came from the pen of Gloria Steinem. This mistress of the sweetest American before–after formula wrote a book called *Revolution from Within. A Book of Self-Esteem*. The 'book', which implies a substitute for all books (like the Book of the Creation of the World), recycles quotations from numerous American Dictionaries of Quotations (where you can find quotations from Hegel to Sartre) and offers a magic personal formula for self-esteem, a new product of the American happiness industry. Between the personal Styron and the personal Steinem, America reinforces its dictatorship of happiness, zealously assuring the individual that happiness is his or her personal choice. And what else could it be? Styron is OK and Steinem is wreathed in smiles.

And her hair is shiny, and neatly cut, and her bestseller was reprinted four times in barely a month. And that makes sacred self-esteem whistle cheerfully and gaily like water from a boiling kettle.

I'm polite here. To every 'How are you today?' I reply: Fine. I no longer even wait to be told, I am the first to say: Have a nice day. I have learned the characteristic intonation as well, the sound that rises brightly like yodelling at the end, a sound which spurs the hearer like a dart, which infallibly raises the level of adrenalin. Have a nice day, I say to myself, but nothing particular happens. I listen. Have a nice day, I repeat. It echoes dully. I chew on emptiness like candy floss, it doesn't taste of anything. There's something missing, I'm aware of a strange longing, which, I assume, is rather like that of dependence.

I walk down Main Street and see him, 'my' Black. He's always here, as though he had grown into the road, he's following his lengthy daily route. His eyes are bloodshot, he talks to himself, waves his arms, keeps stopping, raising his fist, threatening someone who can't be seen, a dangerous type.

I walk behind him as though hypnotized, I just pretend to be going about some business of my own. At first I don't understand what he's saying, and then I make out the word *fuck*. Daga-da-daga-fuck-daga-da-daga-fucking — he marches like a furious human machine. I walk behind him, I follow the compelling bubbles of hatred he leaves behind.

What more could I want, I think, in a country where you can buy a hamburger for 99 cents, and 99 cents are just about 4 quarters, and you can always find 4 quarters. In public telephone boxes which are out of order, you only have to know how, to have the know how ... 4 quarters are a little less than 1 subway token, and you can always find 1 token. If nothing else you can always suck it out, and change it for 5 quarters, you can suck it out of the metal opening in the subway, as the skilful, black subway rats do, the masters, the master token-suckers, the master mother-fuckers ...

I often think of my own people standing around in the main Zagreb square, standing around like penguins, stamping on the asphalt for hours, stamping their dissatisfaction into it, bellyaching ... Bellyaching against the government, bellyaching against their bad luck, belly-aching because at last they've been recognized, bellyach-ing because they have not been recognized by the Polynesians ... Those countrymen of mine bellyache, my home-bred dejected countrymen, you won't easily get a smile out of them, they're quite capable of spitting on the street like llamas in response to your haveanice-day, that's what my own folk are like, those on whose 'life's streets there are many traffic accidents', as Gyorgy Konrad once put it so well and sadly.

'You'll be staying here, won't you?' Americans often ask

me, unshakeably convinced that anything else would be abnormal. And what else could I do? I have come fresh from 'postcommunism', and I've just put the 'iron curtain' into the washing machine, I must have had a bad time, poor thing, waiting in line for toilet paper, what is more I come from a country where people are waving knives over my head, I come from a Balkan bedlam, I've fled from my countrymen from whom you won't easily get a smile, who are capable of spitting on the street like llamas in response to your haveaniceday, I've run away from a country whose life's streets are jammed with traffic accidents... And look at me now! My hair is shiny and neatly cut!

In the meantime I have met 'my' Black. We're sitting on a low wall in front of the shopping centre in Main Street, drinking beer out of a can.

'Don't stay,' says the Black. 'You'll be a Black here like me.'

'That's quite normal for me,' I say. 'Even at home, among my own people, I'm Black.'

'You're right,' says my Black. 'We Blacks are Blacks everywhere.'

'Black is fucking Black everywhere,' I say and feel myself contentedly gurgling somewhere inside: Daga-da-daga-fuck-daga-da-daga-fucking...

'You'll be staying here, won't you?' Americans often ask me, never expecting a negative answer.

'No,' I reply briefly. 'Thank you. I'm unhappy, I'm fine.'

INDIANS

We have sat down on a smooth black rock to smoke a joint. The cigarette is sailing from hand to hand like a silent little ship in the darkness. There are still five minutes to the start. In this grandiose set, hidden by the gloom of Central Park, squatting on the smooth rocks, with the lake in front of us, surrounded by the shimmering magic forest of skyscrapers, our eyes staring at the sky — we seem ethereal. Paul has his arm round his lover, an overgrown boy with long legs like a frog's, slightly protruding dark eyes and full, moist lips, very like Pinocchio. John and Mike are sitting on the rocks, slotting into each other like combs. Marushka and Melisa are standing motionless, hand in hand, their faces turned towards the panorama of Manhattan. The shadows of her parents' genes, ghosts of her Czech mother and Indonesian father, fight for Marushka's face. As though cooling a fever, Marushka plunges her face into Melisa's sandy, expressionless one. Then there are the three of us, Sanja, Goran and I. We rustle, hidden in the darkness, there is no one but us and the forest of skyscrapers clamping Central Park in a golden ring. We smoke our joint, waiting for the fireworks. Another three minutes to the start.

Gazing at the Manhattan panorama, at the shimmering magic forest around us, we wait for the explosion. There are still two minutes to the start... If I were to move the hands of my watch forward six hours, if I turned my eyes to the other side of the sky, a threatening glow would appear on the horizon and I would hear the crack of grenades.

Istria is a peninsula with marvellous mediaeval towns, green valleys, hills and red soil. They say it's full of magnesite. The frequent mists that rise from the valleys and wreathe the mediaeval clock towers are caused, they say, by the magnesite evaporating. There is an exceptionally high proportion of lunatics in Istria, far higher than in other regions of the country. This is also ascribed to the magnesite. Istria has only the middle ages: it's as though it had refused to enter the other centuries. Today's television sets, fridges, satellite antennae are just objects which the magnesite vapours have drawn in from the future. Compasses don't work in Istria. I don't know about watches, but some general time-piece in Istria spins the yarn of time in a way which most definitely does not coincide with ordinary time.

It is not impossible that the Istrian magnesite syndrome has enveloped my whole country like a mysterious mist. It is not impossible that fragments of history are coming back to life, drawn by the magnesite. It is not impossible that the terrible war raging in my country is a replica of wars that have already taken place. Everything has shifted, been displaced, distorted like a crazy compass needle. That is why it is not impossible that camps should suddenly spring up in which former victims torture their tormentors, it is not impossible that on the way I should marry my grandfather whose head was struck off by a sharp blow with an axe, it is not impossible that along the way my father should be my son.

Perhaps this whole mad, postmodern confusion has been caused by magnesite. Perhaps mysterious magnesite currents have drawn different ages into one time, and mixed them all up: sabres, pistols and grenades are all mixed up, turbans with helmets, uniforms with different insignia have all combined, red stars are jumbled up with swastikas, fascists with partisans, Rambos with knights, lasers with daggers, the righteous with the wicked . . . Ages that have come back to life like this are more dangerous and cruel because they have lost their historical logic. The hand which raises the knife has remembered the intensity of the hatred, but it no longer remembers the reason for it, or the aim, in the magnesite madness it is more violent, it strikes twice, seeking double confirmation that it is alive. On the other side of the sky people are going readily to their death, as though it were a video-game: they have already experienced reality once, and reality does not occur twice. People helplessly watch heads being cut off, the memory code is locked in them somewhere, but they no longer know whether the heads that are being cut off are their own or their grandfathers', nor when it is that all this is actually happening. In a madness of haywire clocks the Balkans are sailing like a cursed ship through their own history, dreaming their dreams of war. And for a moment it seems to me that I am sailing into a temporal black hole, into some kind of magnesite senility, I no longer know where I am either: in my future or in my past. Because reality no longer exists.

That's what I'm thinking about as the fireworks burst into the New York sky. On the other side of that sky grenades are exploding and knives flashing. I feel nothing. I don't feel guilty, I don't feel afraid. I'm weightless. My companions are weightless as well. Time is winding and spinning in directions that do not in any case depend on us.

We are standing in a round patch of shade, surrounded by the shadows of bare trees. The sky above us is pink with the glow of the fireworks. We don't speak. We don't know what to do, standing in the dark heart of Central Park like fossils thrown up on the shore by the funnel of time.

And all at once, as though I've been doing it all my life, I suggest to my companions that we dance an Indian dance. How do you do an Indian dance, they ask, eagerly, smiling. And I grab Pinocchio's hand, Pinocchio takes Paul's, Paul Melisa's, Melisa Mike's, Mike

Marushka's . . . *Ha-ya, hayana, ha-ya-na, hayana, hayanaaa,*
we chant in the darkness. I repeat steps I was taught the
previous day, in the streets by an Indian from a reserve
in North Dakota. The steps are my own and so natural
that I might have known them all my life. No one makes
a mistake, no one stumbles, we dance easily, seriously.
We dance in the night, girded by the shimmering forest
of skyscrapers, crammed into the small space of the
tree's shadow. It's cold, our warm breath rises in a mist
from our mouths, as we, Indians, stamp on intently.

MAIL BOX

Dear Duba,

At last I'm writing the letter I promised you, the first after a long spell of complete introversion. I've been a bit preoccupied with learning Dutch, and still more with my need to define my short- or long-term future. It's all as though the dream I used to have often as a child, of going away and never coming back, has come crudely true. But dreams do sometimes invoke the future, and so I have become a foreigner from nowhere, from every-where, an ideal citizen of the world to the local way of thinking here. It doesn't look as if I'll be able to go back ever and I should try to get used to that idea as soon as possible. Expatriation from our common cultural space does after all give one the benefit of a distance I should be thankful for — like something we first feel we

87

should suppress for ever — the ugly face of the past. At the same time it's a step into an enduring European theme — exile, which I now have to recognize as my own personal story.

So far I've had two lives violently interrupted: the first, my island life (seven years in Bol on the island of Brač), and the second, until recently, Belgrade. Belgrade has shattered like the last rotten egg in the Serbian basket and the smell of it has reached me here, although I don't like to admit it. My nostrils are filled with the oppressive odour of the great, general and small, personal apocalypse that has overwhelmed us. I used to be pleased to leave Belgrade, but I was always pleased to get back. Not because it was nicer than any other city in the world for the people who lived there, but because all journeys carry with them the desire to return to the point which possesses us most and in which it's possible to dream about departing, never to return, to a Nowhere Land — somewhere where no one bothers us and where we're absolutely free. But this freedom, which you and I have acquired (because neither the frontiers, nor their inner values, really exist yet in our new states), is not what we actually need. Hence your indecision as to your future movements; it will no longer be a return to a place whose immediately recognizable colours and smells refresh you, preparing you for new flight. It's painful to be completely decentralized. We shall have to get used to it or find a new place to return to, which I find hard to believe in, myself.

As far as your little essays are concerned, I hope you'll

be able to avoid the stereotypes you are so afraid of. Europeans are dumbfounded by America like mountaineers in the desert. It takes a lot of time before first the eyes, and then the imagination, begin to respond to a new influx of values

Since this letter is slipping ever more rapidly down the diverse channels of my agitated thoughts, I'd prefer to be able to talk this all over with you some time, and although it has no real beginning or end, I'll stop here with warm greetings,

P.

Zagreb

Goran is the only one who's all right. The war hasn't affected him particularly, he even finds going down to the shelter interesting, there are a lot of children there he can play war games with. He's very well equipped for war, because I bought him a helmet of the so-called 'Yugoslav People's Army', and a beret like the ones our sailors have at the moment, and all that makes him top dog in the building. H. is writing his book and playing 'Tetris' a lot. That's how he protects himself from the television, which is always on. The problem, as ever, is money. The new notes remind me of Monopoly money. They're so small and nondescript that you spend them without a qualm . . .

It's Saturday morning, S. is in the main room, sitting at the small table in front of the television, a cigarette and a decaffeinated coffee beside her. She's writing you a letter. I asked her to leave me a space to write to you as well. She said: there's not going to be any space, you write your own letter. So I'm sitting at the computer (which is in the bedroom now) writing you my own letter. Goran is in his room, lying on the floor, surrounded by felt-tips, he's writing to you as well — his own letter. Nothing but authorial individualism in this little family workshop in which you are the target audience.

So, I smoke like a skunk, I'm tired as a dog and hungry as a horse. Altogether I've become an interesting sort of animal. What can I tell you — our new state is like a fairy-tale. It's all like Cinderella. A good fairy came, waved a magic wand and turned us into — Europeans. So as to be seen to be so, on television there are female singers dressed up as princesses, and male singers dressed as princes. The ceremonial guard look like tin soldiers. The refugees from Vukovar were taken into the Intercontinental to be filmed for television, and now they're in sports halls, sleeping on mats . . .

When the air-raid warnings stopped, everyday life became easier. That is, it became everyday in a familiar way; astronomical prices, rock-bottom salaries (mine is 200 DM), the cost of living soaring every day.

As far as work is concerned, the situation is incredible. I've made a TV play and four documentaries. None of them has been screened. I'm working on two plays, but

I'm not sure they'll be produced. Otherwise the taxation policy is such that if you earn, say, a hundred thousand, you'll get fifty, so it's hardly worth working. It seems that the best thing is to smuggle, which a lot of people do.

But now there's a new element in people's mood and behaviour. Instead of inflationary hopelessness, people are flailing about, trying to invent ways of finding some kind of income. Your reflexes are different when you're trying to drag yourself bit by bit out of a fundamental evil and when you're falling gradually into — shit. In fact people complain a lot less than before. They have become calculating, resourceful, and when things go wrong they say 'Oh fuck it.' An indication of the increased resourcefulness is the large number of thefts, break-ins and looting. It's not just that war inevitably leads to a breakdown in moral standards, it's also an instinct to get by.

F. told me about a recent bank raid. A masked man went into a bank with a machine gun and shouted: everyone onto the floor! The people looked at him in amazement. He fired a shot into the air and shouted: lie on the floor! The people lay down. Then the man realized there was no one to give him the money. He kicked one poor man on the floor and ordered him to give him money. The man asked: should I crawl? That confused the bank raider and he rushed out of the bank.

I was at the market. Broccoli costs 4 marks, a lettuce almost 8 marks, no one buys bananas any more, not to mention meat of which there are vast quantities. Salaries are about 200 marks and that's considered a good wage. Anything you earn over two hundred is additionally taxed. There are no more imported goods in the shops, so, I warn you, you couldn't buy your cigarettes any more, and I can't get my decaffeinated coffee. If you're lucky you can still get all those things on the coast, there are still imported goods there. In Dubrovnik, indeed, there are Marlboros but no electricity or water.

I'll have to stop now, the letter can't be too fat and I don't know how to turn over the page on the printer (which our neighbour F. has lent us).

Love, H.

Goran is very dependent on me. I can't go anywhere without him asking where I'm going and when I'll be back. I've just sent him away because he was sitting, staring at my letter, which put me off completely. He's just got over flu, which everyone in Zagreb has apart from me. Now I must go and cook lunch, it's my turn today. Do you ever hear from J. in Belgrade? How is she? And the children? If she gets in touch do send her best wishes from us. Warmest greetings from us all, especially the child, who is writing to you himself.

With love, S.

Dear Duba, I really liked the cat you sent me. Next time you write please tell me when you're coming back from America. I've just had flu and I'm still coughing and snuffling but I'm back at school. School is good, it's boring at home.

Lots of love, Goran.

Belgrade

You seem terribly far away, and I miss you more than when you went away on your other trips. The trouble is probably that then life went on in an ordinary way and now there's so much that has changed our lives. Sometimes I feel that all of this could after all settle down, that our lives may once again have at least a firmer framework, sometimes the whole of our past life seems terribly far away, and sometimes I think that it could all somehow renew itself of its own accord . . . I don't know. As you see, the conditional has become part of my style. That's what we wear here, we add it like a stylish touch to what others have designed and sewn for us.

But still when I take stock of everything, I don't have the impression that it's going to be comfortable to live in this part of the world. I'm afraid of the bitterness that has built up in everyone, I'm afraid of the search for proof of loyalty to 'the great ideas' for which we've fought, I'm afraid, in the final analysis, of the material poverty which will mark the life of these lands for years to come. God, how sick it all makes me.

Forgive me for beginning this letter so gloomily, but the war in Bosnia has been raging for several days now. And it doesn't help at all that normal people here, in far greater numbers than anywhere else in this wretched country, have gone onto the streets demanding not to be divided into sheepfolds according to nationality but to be left alone to live peacefully; they went out to the barricades defenceless, thinking that the final and irrefutable argument, but that's a logic which belongs to some other part of the world. Here people shoot at unarmed crowds, those who sought peace have been chased home, and now Bosnia is burning. I don't know what to say, except that I am truly desperate. I hoped it wouldn't come to this. I hoped those blue helmets would be peacefully deployed and we'd manage to reestablish at least some semblance of normal life: that V. would be able to come here, and I would go to Zagreb.

I'm overwhelmed by sorrow and nostalgia for Zagreb, particularly now when everything is seething again and it looks really far away. I remember all the good things that made our lives and wonder whether any of that will exist at all when peace does return, or at least what will be called peace. At the moment what I miss most is contact with all those I love. I can't reach anyone by phone, because you can't get through until after midnight, and then with difficulty, so that I only call V. There wasn't any post for a long time, and it's not reliable now either. I do get a postcard from someone from time to time, but that's so little. And time goes so quickly, I simply can't believe that it's been so long since I left.

It gets worse and worse every day in Bosnia, the future is more and more uncertain. For days now I haven't been able to reach V. by phone and I just hope that this is only temporary. It meant a lot to me just to be able to hear him, to know how he was . . . I don't know how S. and H. are either. If you're in touch with them, send them my love. I'll stop now and go on some other time.

With love, J.

COUCH-POTATO

At the end of January last year I spent a few days in Goteborg. Every day I would go down to the dining-room for breakfast, take a coffee and a roll and settle down in the hotel lobby. Then I would watch the American war reports from Iraq. On the screen the war looked like a video-game, all the more so because the same news was constantly repeated. Indifferent to the war in the Gulf, I sipped my coffee and munched my Swedish roll. I measured the Gulf war in cups of coffee and rolls.

At the end of May last year I found myself in a crowd of people on the main Zagreb square. On the open stage there was a succession of speakers with faces from operetta, girls in traditional costume, musicians and singers. It was very hot, the voices rang harshly in the loudspeakers, the town pigeons flapped their wings nervously in the air. I felt suddenly uneasy and went home, pulled down the blinds and put on the television. You could see everything better on television, but it looked different somehow. The newly elected president was performing an unusual pantomime: he placed a coin in an empty child's cradle, and then released doves of peace. People laid their hands on their chests in the region of their hearts and wept with emotion. At first I thought the pictures were coming from another country, another city, and then I thought they were coming from another age. Only I didn't know whether it was one that had been or one that was yet to come.

I spent last July in my Zagreb flat, behind closed shutters, staring at the television screen. The numbing effect of the pictures reduced the terror which was spreading through the air like an invisible noose. There was a series of Indian films on television. I would turn off the sound and, curled up on my couch, watch Indian women making O shapes with their mouths, gathering their eyebrows into 'V' shapes, whipping Indians with terrible glances, breathing rapidly and looking out of the corner of their eyes, like rabbits. Quite dazed with heat and terror I watched Indian men frowning, folding their arms, sighing, raising their eyebrows in W shapes and whipping the Indian women with glances full of dark longing.

While an invisible noose spread over the town, I lay curled up on the couch, learning Indian gestures, studying the register of Indian emotions as though following a textbook ... I stared at the screen as though at any moment it would emit a distant signal, a message of salvation.

I spent last August in a small island village on the Adriatic. There was just one small cake shop in the village and in it there was a small television set, as big as a large matchbox. In the evening all the locals gathered in the cake shop. The children bought ice-cream loudly; the landlord, an Albanian, juggled the ice-cream balls without taking his eyes from the screen, while we, grown-ups, stood pressed up against one another, hypnotized by the black-and-white picture. Each evening the little screen, no bigger than a large matchbox, poured black-and-white evil over us. The scenes of war looked more terrible on the little television, black-and-white was more terrible than colour, more terrible at night than by day.

I spent last September in my Zagreb flat. A bag with the most essential things stood beside the front door. At the sound of the air-raid siren I would grab my bag and rush down to the cellar. In the cellar I felt like an extra in a war film. In the evening, in my darkened flat, I put on the television and watched houses in ruins, people in tears, human and animal corpses. I often heard gunfire. I would turn down the television so as to hear whether the firing was coming from the street or the television.

I spent last November in New York in a flat belonging to a friend who was away. I hardly left the flat, I watched television. The picture on the screen was often accompanied by the sound of police sirens reaching me from the street.

In December I temporarily rented a little room from Gail in Middletown. On the wall of the little room was a framed letter from Samuel Beckett thanking Gail for choosing him as the subject of her doctoral thesis. Gail was hardly ever at home, so I spent most of my time in the kitchen rather than in my little room. From the little television set, the size of a large matchbox, installed above the dishwasher, came a steady stream of incomprehensible little black-and-white pictures. For some reason I had the feeling the whole time that I was in Moscow. Whether it was because of the yellowing oil paint of the kitchen, or because of time which was passing more slowly, I don't know.

Four years ago, during my last visit to Moscow, I didn't call my Moscow friends as usual. I spent most of the time in my hotel room, hidden behind thick, plush curtains, watching television. On the screen was a succession of shots of Gorbachov, lengthy programmes about the hypnotist Koshpirovsky, who used to hypnotize millions of Soviet citizens over the television, and lingering shots in programmes about how to arrange food tastefully. I stared at the sad sprigs of parsley on the screen and for some reason I felt I was going to die.

Each time I would make it to the end of the broadcast and the weather forecast. The gentle voice of the announcer and the soft music accompanied frozen photographs of Soviet cities in which the mercury had fallen to minus 40 degrees. Lying in my darkened room beside the dim light coming from the screen I thought of Nadezhda Mandelshtam who wrote somewhere that during the Stalinist purges — numb with fear in the face of the invisible Russian roulette whistling over their heads — people spent most of their time lying down.

At the end of December last year I moved into my temporary Middletown flat and immediately ordered cable TV. I moved the couch so that I could watch television lying down. Since then for days I've been watching American women making O shapes with their mouths, and American men gathering their eyebrows into V shapes. I've been learning American gestures, studying the register of American emotions as though following a textbook. American television is like a large classroom for visual instruction.

Some American analyses show that a vast percentage of American children do not distinguish daily life from television reality. It seems that this is not the children's fault. I have some trouble myself. Reality imitates the screen ever more successfully, the screen ever more successfully mimics reality. Besides, reality or screen, it doesn't matter, what matters is to *stay tuned*.

What bothers me is something else. What bothers me is a kind of non-synchronization, a broken connection between the emotional reaction and what provoked the reaction, inappropriate emotions, or something . . . For some time now I have been increasingly aware of mistakes.

In a film a while ago I saw actors leaning over a fresh corpse. Instead of raising their eyebrows anxiously in a V shape, they stretched their faces into a smile. And at the same time they said: terrible, terrible . . . As though they had arrived late, as though they had forgotten to put on the appropriate emotional mask, as though the director had omitted to instruct them.

I saw a programme recently in which ordinary people, contestants, wept over supermarket trolleys crammed with fat turkeys and gigantic packets of detergent, they wept as though they had been affected by an unseen natural disaster. Their faces expressed profound emotion, despite their crocodile tears, they wept sincerely, their bodies shaking. The cause of this powerful emotional reaction was victory in a shopping competition which brought them a few hundred dollars and a trolley full of goods.

Directors anticipate the possible deficiency of the desired response in comedy programmes with 'canned laughter'. Advertisements control any possible deficiency of the correct aesthetic reaction with stern, unambiguous slogans: *This is beautiful!* But what about other emotional reactions? Especially since life imitates the screen, and the screen life?

'How are you?' asks my American friend Norman.

'Terrible,' I reply.

'Fine,' he says, tapping me heartily on the shoulder. 'Oh, I am sorry,' he adds belatedly, raising his eyebrows in a V shape.

Sometimes it seems to me that I have an editing table in my head. I spread out the pictures, correct the spoiled emotional mechanisms. I cut out the shots of the weeping American supermarket contestants and add them to pictures of massacres at home. And so on. I introduce natural order. And then I give up, weary. Who am I, I think, to judge human emotions and correct mechanisms? Besides, I myself have changed, I no longer like it when I get telephone calls from home and they tell me terrible things, when they tell me that 500 shells fell on Osijek that day. How terrible, I say, we've had a heavy snowfall here today . . . And I become aware that I have uttered the sentence quite naturally, without thinking, that my tele-brain has begun to give everything in the world the same heaviness or lightness, everyone the right to an equal number of seconds, everyone his sound-bite, in one shot someone is guzzling a hamburger, in another someone is dying . . . All that matters is to *stay tuned*.

Bela was 29 and Janos Lazar 31 when they closed their door and began to watch television. They did not leave their house for 39 years, said the newspaper article about the couch-potato couple from Savannah. 'We are quite content just watching our TV,' said the Lazars.

I'm lying on my couch, the calendar says it's the end of February. My face has grown grey, I'm drying up inwardly, I am a couch-potato. I think of the way the world is going to the devil, sliding calmly into a white hell of indifference. I think of the fact that the world is nothing but a screen, and we are actors or audience, it doesn't matter which, someone is confidently directing us, and, after all, it doesn't matter. The world is soap-noir, and that is its last genre, a picture which, as it collapses, the globe will keep sending into space like a dead star.

I lie like this, I no longer turn off the television set. Sometimes I wake up at night and smile: the empty screen is looking at me from the corner of the room. From the screen snow drifts into the room. It falls slowly, covering me like a warm blanket. With the last vestige of consciousness I register the gentle voice of the announcer ... In Irkutsk it is minus forty, in Florida plus 30 ... Languages gurgle and merge, smiling and weeping faces slip over one another, the living and the dead, towns coming into being and towns disappearing, geographical points merge, the Amazon runs into the Black Sea, the Volga into the Atlantic ... The globe revolves slowly like an empty screen from which snow drifts ... *Stay tuned*.

YUGO-AMERICANA

I happened to be at a party recently where I shook hands with Lauren Bacall. For Lauren Bacall I was just a silent, anonymous hand. For me her handshake meant far more, among other things the symbolic closing of a cultural circle.

That is, Lauren Bacall could not have known that I came from Yugoslavia and that the culture of my childhood consisted of Greek myths, Partisan tales and — Hollywood films. In the fifties Hollywood films compensated abundantly for the shortage of children's books. Yugoslavia was a country impoverished by war and it seems to have been more expensive to print children's books than to import Hollywood films. As a result, instead of Peter Pan and Winnie the Pooh, other stars shone in the sky of my childhood. Among them Lauren Bacall.

When people do not know the culture of other

countries — which is almost always the case — they replace knowledge with cultural stereotypes. Such a stereotype becomes a little mythic structure, a kind of orientation sign on the cryptic map of the languages, religions, ideologies and cultures of other countries.

Contemporary cultures produce myths about themselves: the strongest media machines produce the most powerful myths. Then when the myth is established it is difficult to make out whether reality produces the cultural myth or the myth reality.

Once established, the cultural myth becomes an object of contention and affirmation, rejection and reinforcement. In short, the myth becomes the basis of a premise in the cultural compound. Like a genre, it generates itself and continues its existence in new cultural products: in films, television, books, fashion, music, art. It seems that cultural myths come into being at the fertile meeting-place of the links between art, popular culture, everyday life, politics, ideology, way of life. And it is precisely those essential links that make them myths and not simply a cultural corpus connected by similar subject-matter.

One of the greatest myths of the twentieth century is Americana, the image America has of itself, which came into being in the middle of the twentieth century somewhere between Hollywood and Madison Avenue. The myth created over the years attained its crowning sophistication in Warhol's painting of the Campbell Soup can and has been repeated ever since in films, novels, television and, again, in life. Today it is not entirely clear whether it is soup that millions of people swallow or — a myth.

The American cultural myth tapped on the doors of postwar Yugoslavia in 1953. That was the year Yugoslav cinemas showed the American film *Water Ballet* with the lovely Esther Williams in the leading role. Esther, of course, had no idea that her beautiful swimmer's leg had symbolically kicked shut the door on an uninvited guest — Soviet Socialist Realism. In 1948 Tito had spoken his famous NO to Stalin, and Esther Williams, the pioneer of the ideological struggle against hardcommunism, served as the most effective propaganda confirmation that Tito was right.

America reached postwar Yugoslavia not only in UNRRA packages, with Truman's eggs, milk and cheddar cheese (I still buy cheddar today out of nostalgia, recalling the orange triangles we were given at school as a snack), but also in Hollywood films. It continued to arrive with translated books: Sinclair Lewis, Upton Sinclair, Theodore Dreiser, John Dos Passos, Irving Stone, Hemingway. In the sixties it came with Kerouacs, Salingers, Ginsburgs. And when television sets entered every house, the screen got smaller, but America got bigger. It poured into every household like longed-for rain: with television series, soap-operas, with Peyton Places, with the McClouds, Dallases, Dynasties and Santa Barbaras.

American culture came as it came: reduced, fragmented, assisted by images from the small and big screens; it came with the media, newspapers, cartoons, music, books, popular culture, symbols, but also with its living media army — returning émigrés, captains of ships, sailors, migrant workers, the children of émigrés. And so it permeated local daily life.

In the fifties, in a small provincial cinema, sitting on a wooden bench without a backrest, my mother held my hand and greedily drank in the images from the screen. At first I didn't understand anything. Later, as a child of eight, I was deeply in love with Audie Murphy, the hero of American Westerns. This small man, who had 22 war-medals for bravery, with his round childish face, was the postwar Yugoslav Superman. When I was ten I callously abandoned Audie, replacing him with Marlon Brando, Brando with James Dean, Dean with Anthony Perkins . . . I remember also the sweet children's commerce in little pictures out of chewing gum packets with portraits of Hollywood actors. Whoever succeeded in filling his or her album possessed unimaginable wealth. Letters were written to Tony Curtis and answers received. Signed photographs were set in places of honour. This was the time of the first Yugo-pop-songs. The texts of these pop-songs abounded in exciting words such as *prairie, cactus, my little horse, revolver, my sweetheart* . . . In the fifties we soaked up everything from the film screen: words, fashion, music, the arrangement of apartments. In that age before off-the-peg clothes, people had their clothes made and women would frequently ask their seamstresses to make a suit like the one Doris Day wore in the film *Pillow Talk*. And the seamstresses knew exactly what kind of suit they meant.

With the appearance of 'Peyton Place', the Yugoslav

television viewer acquired long-lasting entertainment. As a little girl I identified with the character of the teenage girl Alison, played by Mia Farrow. I stepped along the streets of my little provincial town with a notebook forever under my arm, an expression of hysterical alarm on my face.

In local flea-markets you could buy cheap second-hand American goods diligently sent by American émigrés to their poor relations. I gazed enviously at the clothes my friend Lidija had been sent by her émigré grandmother. To make me feel better, my mother bought a little American organdie dress at the flea-market. For some unknown reason, it was like an Austrian dirndl. And when my friend received a large parcel containing a worn red windcheater with a hood and her first jeans, my heart broke definitively with envy. With those jeans and her red windcheater, my friend could have had any boy she wanted.

Perhaps the history of the American myth in postwar Yugoslav culture can best be illustrated by small details: the first postwar translations of American books abounded in footnotes. Everything had to be explained: what a juke box was, what marijuana was, and what jeans were. The footnotes (of the type: *juke box*, a machine that plays music when a small coin is put into it) began to disappear, gradually at first, then ever more rapidly, because these unknown things were becoming more and more a part of everyday reality. The world had evidently become a global village. Perhaps it had become a global American village, but we needn't go into that here. All in all, the same films began to be shown at the same time in cinemas in New York and Zagreb, my mother and my American friend Norman's mother, Edith, watched 'The Golden Girls' on television simultaneously.

Besides, in a way people began to resemble one another. In the film *Working Girl* I was touched by Melanie Griffith's friend with her pink-and-light-blue nylon wedding, so like our own weddings. I was overcome by a feeling of deep understanding in the scene in which the two of them, looking through their rich boss's wardrobe, find an elegant black dress. 'That must have cost six hundred dollars!' says Melanie in awe. 'And it's not even leather!' says her friend, disappointed.

I felt a pang when I heard the malicious Alexis rebuke her lover in a scene from 'Dynasty'. In a luxurious bath they are drinking champagne and eating caviar. At one moment Alexis cries out: 'Hey, go easy, that's caviar you're eating!' The remark was not intended for her lover, but for the millions of Americans who had to be reminded of one more stereotype of wealth. I was touched by the thought of those for whom the television screen really was a window into a more beautiful, better, more brilliant world. Norman's mother in Detroit and my mother in Zagreb were in that sense equal inhabitants of the global village.

Perhaps it was this same sense of vague global brotherhood that drove my colleague Pavle Pavličić to write a short story entitled 'Return to Hannibal'. The story was published in the eighties and describes parallel

109

worlds, little Hannibal on the Mississippi and little Vukovar on the Danube. Hannibal and Vukovar are like connected vessels, the houses are the same, the people are the same, lives and events unfold in them, in parallel. Everything that happens in Vukovar on the Danube occurs at the same time in Hannibal on the Mississippi.

Today, just under four years later, the story which until recently had no fantastic dimension is no longer plausible. Because if the logic of reality were to follow the logic of Pavličić's short story, Hannibal on the Mississippi would have today to be razed to the ground. In just one year reality has brutally destroyed the idea of the sameness of various worlds. Once long ago some bloody reality produced the Balkan Myth, today it is the Balkan Myth that is producing our bloody reality.

Unpredictable reality continues its game with myths. From here I observe the media reinforcement of the Balkan Myth as it is gradually built up from newspaper photographs and television reports. The television shots of desperate, wretched, dishevelled people with wild eyes absolutely coincide with the Balkan stereotype. And no one asks how it is that many of these desperate people have a decent command of the English language. At the same time as the myth of the wild Balkans is being composed here (after all, reality does not suggest any alternative), in the Balkans themselves people continue to live — the American myth! Balkan reality refuses to conform to its own image, it prefers the American one! And so in slang a knife is called a rambo, Croatian soldiers wear bands round their foreheads like Sylvester

Stallone, the town of Knin is known as Knin Peaks, and the Serbian paramilitary groups are Kninjas. Reality is swiftly immortalized not only in newly composed songs in the style of the oral epic tradition, but also in the deeply American genre of strip cartoons. Murderers like the Serbian Captain Dragan are today the heroes of cartoons; they carry a knife in their hands and on their feet they wear Reeboks! In Belgrade slang, Belgrade is now known as Arkansas. Arkan is the name of a murderer, a confectioner by trade, a famous hunter of Croatian heads.

And then again, at the same time as I watch horrific American television pictures of the destruction of Sarajevo, my mother in Zagreb is watching 'Santa Barbara'. And while tanned actors utter their lines, their expressions numbed with boredom, comprehensive promiscuity and moving around in a confined space, warning subtitles often run across the screen: air-raid danger in Zadar, air-raid danger in Karlovac, air-raid danger in Slavonski Brod . . .

Balkan reality, then, does not identify with the Balkan Myth but, once again, with the American one. The difference is only in death, the real, homegrown, Balkan kind. At the same time many Americans still believe that deaths 'down there' in the Balkans are celluloid deaths. Not all of them do, of course. Not Lauren Bacall.

SUSPECT

On Wednesday 1.22.1992, at approximately 4.27 pm, a female Wesleyan student was walking in the vicinity of Wyllys Avenue. An unidentified male approached her from behind and lifted up her skirt. The male then fled.

The suspect is described as Caucasian, of small to medium build, with short cropped hair and no facial hair. He was wearing a leather jacket and blue jeans. The description of the suspect matches descriptions in other incidents reported in the last school year.

Anyone having any information in regard to this incident is asked to call Wesleyan Public Safety, at 347–9411.

On Saturday 2.1.1992, at approximately 10.49 pm, a female Wesleyan student was walking along William Street in the area between High and William streets. A male jumped out of a nearby bush and struck the woman several times in the face. The male then fled in the direction of William Street, while the woman shouted for help.

The suspect is described as African-American, tall, about twenty years old. He was wearing a grey jacket, blue jeans and white sneakers.

Anyone having any infomation in regard to this incident is asked to call Wesleyan Public Safety, at 347–9411.

Several female students have reported incidents of sexual contact in the vicinity of the campus. In all cases a male has approached the women from behind, grabbing them by the hips. The suspect then fled.

Last semester similar incidents were reported in the area between Washington Street and Broad Street.

The suspect is described as Caucasian, of medium build, with dirty blond shoulder-length hair.

Anyone having any information in regard to the reported incidents is asked to call Wesleyan Public Safety, at 347–9411, ext. 2596, or the Middletown Police department at 347–6941.

On Monday 2.17.1992, at approximately 10.02 pm, two female Wesleyan students were walking along Washington Street when an unidentified male approached them from behind and grabbed one of the women round the hips, with both hands. The suspect then fled the area.

The suspect is described as Caucasian, of thin build, with light brown hair and freckles. He was wearing tan pants and a blue hooded sweatshirt which was pulled tightly over his head.

Anyone having any information in regard to this incident is asked to call Wesleyan Public Safety, at 347–9411.

On Friday 2.22 at approximately 12.40, a female Wesleyan student was walking along Loveland Street. A male approached her from behind and grabbed her pocketbook. The woman fought her attacker as she tried to run away. During the struggle the male made sexual contact with the woman.

The suspect is described as African-American, strong, of medium build. He was wearing a short-sleeved shirt.

Anyone having any information in regard to this incident is asked to call Wesleyan Public Safety, at 347–9411.

On Friday 2.29 at approximately 4.00 pm, three Wesleyan students were in the Indian Hill Cemetery off Vine Street. The students were approached by a male who initially asked them for money. Upon the students telling the suspect that they did not have any money, the suspect alleged that he had a gun and demanded that they give him a camera that the students were using. The suspect took the camera and fled.

The suspect is described as an African-American male, 5'7", 130 lbs, medium build with short-cropped hair. The suspect was wearing light-colored jeans and a brown leather jacket.

Anyone with any information in regard to this incident is asked to call Wesleyan Public Safety at 347–9411, ext. 2596, or the Middletown Police department at 347–6941.

On Tuesday 3.3.1992, a female Wesleyan student was taking a shower in the women's locker room of the Freeman Athletic Center. An unidentified male entered the women's locker room and pulled aside the plastic shower curtain. The male looked at the woman for several seconds, and then fled.

The suspect is described as Caucasian, of small to medium build, with fair hair and blue eyes. He was wearing grey trousers and a T-shirt pulled half-way up his face.

Anyone having any information in regard to this incident is asked to call Wesleyan Public Safety, at 347–9411.

On Thursday 3.5.1992, at approximately 2.23 pm, a female Wesleyan student was walking along College Street, eastwards from High Street. An unidentified male grabbed the woman by the skirt and then fled.

The suspect is described as Hispano-American, with brown hair, of medium height. He was wearing a leather jacket, blue jeans and white sneakers.

Anyone having any information in regard to this incident is asked to call Wesleyan Public Safety, at 347–9411.

On Friday 3.12.1992, at approximately 4.40 pm, a male entered a non-university building on Brainerd Avenue, where he attacked a non-university female. The male grabbed the woman by the neck and threatened her.

When a resident entered the building, the suspect took fright and fled. The suspect is described as African-American, of tall build. He was wearing a blue baseball cap with a red symbol and a blue-and-white striped shirt.

Anyone having any information in regard to this incident is asked to call Wesleyan Public Safety, at 347–9411.

On Monday 3.16.1992, at approximately 2.56 pm, a female Wesleyan student was walking down High Street. An unidentified male approached her and grabbed her by the breasts, first the left and then the right. The male then left the area.

The suspect is described as Asiatic, of short build, with dark hair and dark eyes. At the time of the attack, he was wearing blue jeans, a jacket with the Wesleyan University crest and white sneakers.

Anyone having any information in regard to this incident is asked to call Wesleyan Public Safety, at 347–9411.

On Wednesday 3.18.1992, at approximately 10.45 pm, a female Wesleyan student was leaving the North College building.

The woman encountered an unidentified male who forced her to take cover behind the wall of the college on the north side, where he abused her sexually. During the attack the woman succeeded in striking her assailant and fleeing.

The suspect is described as Caucasian, approximately twenty years old. He was wearing a baseball cap with *New York Knicks* written on it and a jacket with *Raiders* on the back.

Anyone having any information in regard to this incident is asked to call Wesleyan Public Safety, at 347–9411.

On 3.19.92 at approximately 6.30 pm, a female Wesleyan student was taking a shower in her residence hall near Church Street. Three males entered the bathroom and one male looked in the shower stall. The student informed the male it was a women's bathroom and the males left the area.

The males are described as African-American, approximately thirteen to sixteen years of age. The male who looked into the shower stall was wearing a full-length red wool coat. The second male was wearing a black hooded *Raiders* jacket. There is no description available on the third male.

Anyone having any information in regard to this incident is asked to call Wesleyan Public Safety at 347–9411, ext. 2596.

On Thursday 3.26.1992, a female, a tenant of the university building on Court Street, brutally raped an IBM typewriter, electric, university property. The incident was reported by a male, a tenant of the same building, a member of the university, stating that he was awoken at approximately 1.32 am by 'a perverse noise'.

The suspect is Caucasian, a foreigner, she belongs to the teaching staff of Wesleyan University, she wears jeans and Reebok sneakers, and is of medium to tall build. The suspect maintains that she is a writer, that she did indeed commit 'rape', but of her text, not the typewriter.

As university property is our responsibility, anyone who knows anything about similar incidents is asked to report them, by calling 347–9411.

BODY

Golden-yellow orange juice glistens in a sunlit glass; a thick, sweet layer of caramel slides down hillocks of pinkish ice-cream; with a ripping sound the zip on a pair of jeans makes its way up towards a belly-button bedewed with golden droplets of sweat; a juicy behind displays its pear-shaped form; thick ketchup drips, drenching thirsty pasta; pearly teeth sink into an apple with a juicy crunch; waterfalls of silky curls cascade down delicate female shoulders; little flakes of oats fall with a silent crash into a milky sea with porcelain shores; and it's all so *juicy*, ah, all so *crispy*, mmm, all so *crunchy*, mmmm, all so *fluffy*, mmmm, all so *delicious*, ohhh, it is all so *irresistible*.

I adore American TV-ads. American TV-ads are the condensed, perfectly designed ideology of American daily life. They articulate and at the same time nurture the fundamental substance of American life. And the fundamental substance of American life (and every other life, only no one else has realized it!) is the body. The BODY! The eating, walking, sleeping, moving body. This straightforward message — the b-o-d-y — pours out of television screens sprinkled through a multicoloured carnival of images.

American ads articulate and at the same time nurture each part of the body in turn. Most frequently and above all they appeal to — the mouth. They recommend which little flakes Americans should propel into their mouths, which biscuits they should munch on, which canned food they should consume, which drinks they should swallow, which sweets they should nibble. They teach Americans how to feed their bodies.

If one group of ads concerns itself assiduously with *filling*, another is zealously occupied with — *emptying*. Advertisements dealing with uncomfortable gripes alternate with ads for hamburgers, advertisements for unpleasant gases with ads for sweets, advertisements for laxatives with ads for juices, advertisements for haemorrhoids with those for cheeses.

While one group of ads treats the body like a machine for digesting food, another is concerned with the way to bring this sated body to its optimal form: how to slim it down, how to divest it of superfluous fat, how to shape it, how to make it dynamic (*Move your body!* commands one slogan), how to train it, how to bring it to perfection.

With touching seriousness, the American celebrity Jane Fonda advertises her very own discovery — a small, cheap, plastic step for shaping the leg muscles — with just the same touching seriousness as she once protested against the war in Vietnam.

If a photograph in the *New York Times* of a beautiful body with the caption 'Body Consciousness' (whatever that means) is several times larger than a photograph of fresh corpses somewhere in Bosnia, then it is quite n-o-r-m-a-l that an American (and this happened to me) should do exercises while you are answering his question about 'that war in the Balkans'. Or that the person you are talking to (this happened to me as well) should leap up from her chair in a restaurant and quite naturally perform a few exercises for stretching the spine while you are talking about postmodernism in which she, the person you are talking to, is otherwise passionately interested.

Work on the body is not yet finished. American TV-ads also offer Americans abundant advice as to how they should cherish their sated and beautifully exercised body — *Nourish it inside, nourish it outside* recommends one ambiguously rhythmic TV slogan. Advertisements talk about skin, hair, teeth, legs, face. American TV screens gush with bath foams, shampoos, perfumes, creams.

Hearing that I was from 'Eastern Europe', one American woman immediately asked me eagerly 'Do you have Body Shops over there?'

My student Alyosha from Irkutsk told me a story. Before students from the (former) Soviet Union began to disperse through American universities, the American organizers of the exchange programme arranged a kind of short briefing for them. The American side gave each student a bar of soap, a towel, deodorant and a sheet of paper with instructions about behaviour in America. In the first paragraph it said that Americans were a 'clean' people, that they took showers every day (several times!) so the Soviet students were asked to follow that pattern themselves, to use deodorants and change their under-wear every day.

There is, therefore (clean) America and — *the others*. At the frontier between these two worlds I imagine Woody Allen as the customs officer. Why him? Because some-where he described a nightmare in which some people broke into his flat in order to — shampoo him!

Work on the body is still not finished. Now your immediate surroundings have to be put in order. There are numerous advertisements recommending to Ameri-cans how to clean the space around them: what to use for the kitchen, the bathroom, furniture, windows, dishes, clothes, what to use for the lavatory bowl. This group awakens in the female viewers a deeply rooted, childish dream about a dolls' house, so it is no wonder that one New Yorker who was renting an apartment to a countryman of mine should have shown him a pillow-case and sheet and said in a didactic tone: 'This is a pillowcase, we, Americans, put it on the pillow, and this is a sheet, we, Americans, put it on the bed.'

And when at last everything is clean — inside and out — American ads advise Americans to place their sated, exercised, nurtured body — in a car.

The only advertisement that is concerned with the non-corporeal sphere of American life is the one that teaches Americans how to telephone most effectively and cheaply! Other human activities, to judge by TV-ads, of course, are quite insignificant. There are just a few advertising messages concerning travel (recreation of the body!), which credit cards to choose (in order to pay for everything the body has consumed), and so on.

In American culture the body is treated as His Excellency the Body. The American ideology of the body will therefore do all it can to remove and destroy the old-fashioned, shameful *multiple meanings,* which the idea of the body implies. So it is that the bald, and then immediately abundantly hirsute, men who move over the TV screen are devoid of even the slightest hint of parody: advertisements for wigs and hair-transplants are advertisements like any others. Advertisements with well-endowed beauties will slip past shots of thousands of silicone breasts removed and thrown onto piles, but it will not occur to anyone to make an ironic connection between the shots. Alongside ads for gleaming teeth there are ads for artificial denture gum: the perfect design of both destroys any notion of an ironic contrast.

In its ideology of the body, America deprives the body of the right to its carnival-grotesque ambivalence. The TV screen will carry shots of a contest to find the fattest American woman or the ugliest face in America, but the television — that potent shaper of collective thinking — will destroy every ironic-subversive message. The contest for the fattest American woman will not be interpreted as the carnival revolt of the ugly body against the beautiful, or at least as its logical opposite, it will rather resemble the democratic permission of democratic America to allow the existence of alternatives, of variants. But the participants in the contest themselves will not behave as ugly, but as *alternatively beautiful* women.

Notions which have sprung from this same ideology will be devoid of irony as well, no matter how bizarre they are: notions of the hibernation of the body, of the mummification of the body, and so on. So, for instance, the lawyers in 'L.A. Law' will treat with the utmost seriousness the case of a client who wishes to be mummified after his death!

In its ideology of the unambiguous body America has decisively removed all its opposites: illness, ageing, death, ugliness, physical decay. As a deeply infantile culture, America builds its ideology of the body on infantile mechanisms (besides, is it only the body that needs sophistication?). This collective American body is like a baby that feeds, burps, shits, pees, takes its first steps — and receives the enthusiastic acclaim of its surroundings. Almost all advertisements satisfy the infantile level of existence: the most explicit is, for example, the one promoting measures to counteract diarrhoea (or constipation, it doesn't matter). The husband is leaving for work with a worried look on his face, his wife, with an expression that 'knows and understands everything', hands him some pills. In the next shot the husband telephones home from work: all traces of offended annoyance have been wiped from his face: he is smiling, relaxed, confident (he doesn't have to keep running to the bathroom). Bravo, his wife's face applauds. Bravo, the millions of American TV viewers applaud.

Every bodily victory in the American pioneering myth, 500 years old and still juvenile, receives the approval of its surroundings. Michael Jackson, a living rubber doll, symbol of the American body designing and re-designing itself, metamorphosing, turning from black to white, a body reaching for eternity — receives general applause. Bravo, Michael, bravo, victorious body.

Willard Scott, a centenarian who goes to a dancing class every day, coquettishly sticking out her old-lady's belly, earns the applause of America. 'What's the secret of living so long?' Americans ask Willard Scott. And it doesn't occur to anyone to ask what the purpose is: 'What's the point of living so long?' Longevity is an end in itself. Bravo, Willy! Bravo, long-living body!

Women and men who go in for body-building — called beefcakes almost without irony — earn the applause of their surroundings. Bravo, body!

In the most crowded New York streets, you can see a lone young man stop, put down his bag, take out his weights and start pumping. At night in New York you can see individuals in sports clothes stopping beside walls, steps, concrete blocks, stretching their bodies, taking no notice of anything or anyone. These isolated exercisers exercise their muscles in the New York night. And it seems they need no one, they appear self-sufficient. Perhaps they emit signals unconsciously, perhaps the trembling of their muscles, carried through the light years, will provoke a slight vibration on some other planet. The isolated muscle pulsates in the New York night, sending its signals into the unknown.

These isolated exercisers, samurai warriors, who have abandoned the sanctioned places — fitness centres, parks, beaches, open and closed exercise areas — and dispersed throughout American space simply radicalize the idea of the beautiful, healthy, dynamic and autistic body. For the American body does not communicate with anyone and does not serve any purpose.

That is to say, the American ideology of the body has deprived this alluring body of its right to association, to its sexual function, it has deprived this sexually attractive body of its right to sexual attraction. This deprivation of function has been institutionalized by the law on harassment: every thought, even the most innocent, of the sexual use of the body has become an offence. And the mental castration of the sexual function has liberated space for new functions.

A new advertisement for Reebok sports shoes promotes a strong and independent female body, ready for the hardest physical exploits. *Life is short, play it hard*, advises the slogan. The advertisement seems to suggest a new function for the body, a warlike one. As though some future America will be ruled by strong women-warriors who will wear Reeboks instead of armour.

The mental castration of the sexual function of the body opens up space for new aesthetic functions. The asexual body becomes — a sculpture. The rejected fetish of the bust (bequeathed by bountiful nature or silicon) has been replaced today by the fetish of the arm, for which we are ourselves responsible. Like every *objet d'art*, the sculptured arm soon found its promoters, its philosophers, critics, its artistic workshops. 'Self-determination,' says Radu, the artistic director of a studio for physical culture in Manhattan. 'Discipline and power,' recommends Pasquale Manocchia, Madonna's personal trainer. Pump-up aesthetics, self-determination, are the new terms, and bodily beauty is undergoing redefinition. 'Beauty today is the muscle in motion — living, active, graceful matter, like a cobra,' says Radu the aesthete.

In the altered, sexually castrated or simply new system of values, it can happen that a glance at a turkey, plump as a harem beauty, lying outspread (always on its back!) in the freezers of American supermarkets, can make one blush, and the sight of a built-up muscle makes the mouth water! Is there something wrong? And is that not why the harem turkey is vainly wrapped in polythene packaging which, in fact, simply emphasizes its roundness? Is there something wrong? Everything's fine. One of the logical notions produced by the American system of distorted functions of the body is — cannibalism. If the body must not serve certain functions, why shouldn't it serve others? Besides, who would dream of eating a starving African child, a yellow Chinaman, a desiccated Turk who smokes a hundred cigarettes a day, or a wretched man who has been massacring people in the Balkans? But the American body, beautiful, healthy and so pointless ... with those biceps and triceps, lively, active and graceful as cobras ... Mmm, that's so juicy, mmmm, so fluffy, so crispy, mmm, irresistible ...

After all, the substitution of the whole by the part, the body by the fetish of the arm, satisfies the gourmet principles of cannibalism. No cannibal up to now has ever eaten the whole body, not even Chikatilo.

Andrei Chikatilo, the Russian cannibal who ate 56 people between 1978 and 1990, was given tremendous publicity in the American media. 'I am a mistake of nature, a mad beast,' proclaimed the cannibal from Rostov in the American version. Chikatilo went on to announce that his cannibalism was a result of 'sexual inadequacy and the repressive Soviet system'. Chikatilo (together with George Bush) not only delivered the final blow to communism, but introduced a new, political aspect to the sophisticated American cannibalism of silent lambs and American psychos.

His Excellency the Body ...

I come from a country in which the body is just a cheap target. When I got here, of course, I immediately rushed off to an aerobics class, ordered a Nordic Track, filled my kitchen cupboards with Slim-Fast, and I've got a thigh-master rolling around pornographically in a corner. And then I realized it was too late and gave up. I'm too old, indoctrinated, used to the idea that the body isn't worth anything, that it's just a cheap target. Everyday reality in my terrible country confirms this constantly. In my country human bodies are used to fertilize the soil, to feed chickens and pigs, bodies fill pits so that the fat black seed of evil may one day spring from them again.

Actually, I didn't quite give up.

A little while ago, I read an advertisement in my local newspaper. Roger Papazian from nearby Rocky Hill was advertising an unusual service in his workshop 'Eden' . . .

And so, when I die, please cremate me, and then place my ashes not in an urn, but in the hands of Mr Papazian. He promises that he will use my ashes to fill bullets. I, an incorrigibly idle slob, will at last have a satisfactory body: slim, light, seductive, aerodynamic and dangerous. At last I shall be 'narrow as an arrow'! And where I end up — in the heart of an aged lover, in the body of an enemy, or some innocent wild duck — is quite unimportant. Because the body is eternal. Only the spirit is perishable.

HARASSMENT

As a foreigner in America I had a lot of difficult things to work out. I worked out how to use coupons for super-market shopping (a real nightmare for any East Euro-pean foreigner!); I managed to grasp how to shop by television, telephone and catalogue; how to use the famous 1–800 numbers; how to react when the manic voice of an answer-phone instructs you how to call another answer-phone; I learned how to make collect-calls; and even how and why to change telephone com-panies. I sussed out a few things about taxation, a source of terrible headaches not only for foreigners but for Americans as well; I made out how to use cash-dis-pensers. I no longer push my fingers into the sink outlet if the propeller blades for shredding garbage are switched on, I worked that out too. I switched off the fire alarm as soon as I moved in. I smoke and I know how sensitive they are to smokers. I sussed that out too.

I can identify with many major American problems. Hate-crimes, for instance, crimes committed out of pure hatred, which are incomprehensible to Americans, but I am entirely familiar with them. I think I can make out the problems of American intellectualism and anti-intellectualism, the feminization of American culture and its renewed masculinization. What is mainstream, what American classes are, the American electoral system, the culture of American daily life, none of this is unfamiliar to me. I understand everything that begins with multi (multicultural, multinationalism and multimillionaires); everything with ism, from adhocism to consumerism; I understand everything post, from postcommunism to postcolonialism. I understand new age, self-esteem, virtual reality, New World Order, globalization and similar things. I'm even beginning to get the hang of American baseball, which is incomprehensible to many foreigners.

There's only one thing I can't make out: harassment. The fact that my English-Croatian dictionary explains that harassment means torment, annoyance, irritation, disturbance and constant attack doesn't tell me much. I'm grateful to an American colleague who kindly gave me instructions, a leaflet with illustrations, so that even the illiterate should understand, but I still don't! Studying the leaflet I realized for instance that harassment is divided into verbal, non-verbal and physical abuse. Verbal harassment consists of: threats and insults, offensive or suggestive comments, messages of sexual content, insisting on intimate meetings, offensive jokes and teasing, whistles and catcalls of various kinds. Non-verbal harassment includes suggestive gestures or looks, winking and indecent licking of the lips, then the distribution of placards, photographs or drawings of a sexual nature. Physical harassment includes rape or attempted rape, pressing another person into a corner or against a wall, pinching, shoving or slapping, then touching, embracing and kissing.

The explanations that define the difference are not, I must say, altogether clear to me. My instructions define verbal harassment indistinctly. It could be harassment, it says, if someone insists on a meeting even if you have said 'no'. It seems that it is not sexual harassment if someone invites you out and accepts your 'no' answer. Non-verbal harassment confuses me too. It could be sexual harassment, say the instructions, if a person stares at your body often, but it is probably not a question of sexual harassment if a person stares at you as you pass by. As far as physical harassment is concerned the situation is far clearer. The difference is in the regularity. My instructions state that it is physical harassment if someone regularly rubs against us, but it is, probably, not if the same or some other person happens to bump into us.

This, sexual, harassment is a dangerous thing because it can take several different forms, say my instructions. And so I am constantly on my guard. For instance, I don't want sexual harassment to affect my working ability. Certainly not. The instructive sketch that gets to me most is the picture of a woman worker wearing a protective helmet. And while in a bubble above her head there is a clock with wings, i.e. she is thinking of the way time is flying by, above the head of her colleague, also in a helmet, is a bubble of quite different content: a table for two in a restaurant! If I ever meet such a type with a protective helmet on his head and fantasies about restaurants above it, and if he starts persuading me to go out with him, if he keeps giving me presents, if he makes offensive comments about my appearance and clothes (especially if we bear in mind that I have a helmet on my head!), if he touches me in a way I find disagreeable (rather than agreeable), if he tells me sexy jokes and keeps hanging up posters with sexual messages in my vicinity, I have the right to take a swine like that straight to court. That's what my instructions guarantee.

On the other hand, I'm not entirely sure that Americans quite understand the instructions. I observe that to be on the safe side they don't look at the person they are talking to for more than three seconds. And I have got into their way of timing myself. I keep lowering my eyes. I've become paranoid. I don't lick my lips even when I'm eating pancakes with maple syrup, my favourite American treat. The thing is, I don't know how people around me would interpret my action. I have become sensitive to every kind of physical abuse. For instance, for days I was harassed by the bathroom door handle. I would walk past and the handle would grab me by the sleeve every time. It infuriated me so I unscrewed it and threw it in the garbage. That loathsome harassing handle!

I'm lonely. I don't invite anyone to my place. I don't accept invitations. You never know. All kinds of harassment can be lying in store for you round any corner. That's one of the reasons why I like New York. I can secretly live out my desires there. I go into the overcrowded subway, mix with the people, I like all that shoving and pressing. I especially like the subway on rainy days: I enjoy that mixing up of anonymous coats moist with rain. I let my gaze roam freely over the faces, I carry out secret harassment, enjoying the New York faces, so varied, so un-similar. The New York subway is the biggest stage of un-similar faces in the world. On the escalators I wink at one person, blow a kiss into the air. My kiss floats upwards or downwards and lands on someone like a soft little feather. I adore New York crowds, I rub up against someone's shoulder, someone rubs against me, I touch someone in passing, I collect touches like matches. *Touch to touch* . . . So as not to be cold in Middletown.

Because I do feel cold in Middletown. Smaller places are more assiduous in following rules of behaviour. As I go along Court Street, I see a mother taking a walk with her little son. They are enjoying the cold, sunny day. I look at the little boy's pale profile, there's something touching about the child.

'What's your name?' I ask, in a friendly way.

'I don't talk to strangers,' says the boy looking solemnly straight ahead.

'Oh . . .?' I say.

'I don't talk to strangers,' the child repeats, looking straight ahead.

'Interesting . . .' I say.

'I don't talk to strangers,' the child repeats persistently.

'I'm sorry, lady,' his mother joins in solemnly, 'don't talk to him. I've taught him not to talk to anyone he doesn't know. Too many horrible things are happening, you know.'

'I understand, I'm sorry,' I mumble and hurry away.

So ready to find in every little thing some general, obsessive topic, to dissect it collectively, to take it to its extreme conclusion, extreme instances, to articulate and define it, to institutionalize it — whether it is a question of D-Day, catastrophes, jaws, earthquakes, parasites, cancerous rays, unicorns or Aids — Americans are for the moment obsessively preoccupied with sexual harassment and the sexual abuse of children.

It seems to me, a foreigner forgetting for a moment where I'm from, that America is living through all the myths of all the cultures that came into being before her; that she is experiencing them passionately, collectively, in a fairy-tale, ignorant mish-mash, where the origin quoted is not important, what matters is the story. It seems to me that in America any theme that has the structure of myth, a primordial form, a fairy-tale, an archetype, really flourishes. Myth is a fable, American culture is fabulous, American culture is profoundly mythic. So it is not at all clear (and not at all important) whether the theme of sexual harassment has been brought to the surface by genuine and, they say, alarming statistics, or whether it is just the infantile longing of collective America for a new myth, a new collective psychoanalytical theme. Or both. Such a theme is readily taken up by the media, the newspapers, publishing houses, television, the film industry, it becomes a public, collective and personal nightmare, it determines behaviour, attitudes, it stimulates new laws, like adrenalin it quickens the collective American metabolism, sharpens the sensibilities, clarifies attitudes.

But if I, a foreigner, for a moment remember where I'm from, I am suddenly ashamed, and then I think that America is profoundly right. Because the history of the Balkan countries is nothing but the history of mutual harassment. 'This nation has suffered too much', writes Ivo Andrić, the only Yugoslav Nobel Prize-winner, 'from disorder, violence and injustice and is too used to bearing them with a muffled grumble, or else rebelling against them, according to the times and circumstances. Our people's lives pass, bitter and empty, among malicious, vengeful thoughts and periodic revolts. To anything else, they are insensitive and inaccessible. One sometimes wonders whether the spirit of the majority of the Balkan peoples has not been for ever poisoned and that, perhaps, they will never again be able to do anything other than suffer violence, or inflict it.'

When I think about all of that my Middletown coldness begins to appeal to me. You're right, lady, don't let your child talk to strangers! And how good it would be, I go on thinking, if I could take many of my Balkan countrymen to court. For harassment, for one of the bloodiest examples of harassment of our times.

EEW

I envy 'Western' writers. I see my colleague, a Western writer, as an elegant passenger travelling without luggage.

I see myself as a passenger travelling with an enormous amount of luggage, a passenger trying desperately to get rid of his burden, but it drags tenaciously after him like destiny itself.

My Zagreb dentist with 'a natural talent for inflicting pain' asked me several months ago what I was doing in his clinic, that is: why was I not at the front.

'How do you mean?'

'You're a writer, aren't you?'

'I seem to be.'

'Then you ought to be at the front. To get some idea of what blood looks like!'

'I'm afraid of blood.'

'You're afraid? At a time when people are dying for the homeland you sit here calmly having your caries filled and announce that you don't care for blood!' shouted my Zagreb dentist, angrily waving his drill over my head.

It was several months ago, in the dentist's chair, that it first occurred to me that all my life I had been doing everything in my power to retain my right to my one single privilege. The privilege of being a writer. I refused to be a member of any parties, organizations, commissions and juries, I avoided being left or right, upper or lower. I was a damned outsider. I refused membership of mountaineering, feminist or diving clubs. I believed that a writer should have no homeland or nation or nationality, a writer must serve neither an Institution nor a Nation, neither God nor the Devil, a writer must have only one identity: his books, I thought, and only one homeland: Literature (where did I get that idea?).

Alarmed by so powerful an argument as the dentist's drill, I admitted that the dentist was right and left the country. If I could do nothing for my homeland, I thought, at least I could preserve my right to freedom — I would fight for the right of my writing not to serve anyone or anything, apart from itself. My Literature, my Belles Lettres, I repeated to myself, clutching my only ID — my books — in my hand . . .

As soon as I crossed the border, the customs officers of culture began roughly sticking identity labels on me:

communism, Eastern Europe, censorship, repression, Iron Curtain, nationalism (Serb or Croat?) — the very labels from which I had succeeded in protecting my writing in my own country.

'What do you think about communism?' an American journalist asked me. 'I know, it was terrible,' she said emotionally, screwing up her face, 'but in a transitional period the phenomenon itself seeks re-articulation . . .'

I listened to her, not believing my ears. How did she know it was *terrible*, and how easily all those words: communism, transition, postcommunism tripped off her tongue.

'I'm not a politician, I'm a writer,' I said.

'I'm asking you because you're a writer, an intellectual, the representative of a postcommunist country . . .'

God, I thought, if she only knew that in my country writers, taking on the role of politicians, were as responsible for the war as the generals, because when they were asked the same questions they were only too eager to answer.

'We're talking about literature,' I said.

'Let's leave boring questions about literature to Western writers. As an East European writer and intellectual you surely have far more interesting things to talk about than literature.'

At gatherings here I sometimes come across colleagues of mine, 'Easterners', EEWs (East European Writers), and see how they have adapted in advance to the given stereotype, how readily they chatter about censorship (although they've had no experience of it themselves). I hear them babbling on about postcommunism, about the everyday life of their sad Eastern Europe, talking about democracy in transition, proposing measures for getting out of the crisis (from nationalism to agriculture!), eagerly accepting identity tags, wearing them like badges, sticking together — Russians with Hungarians, Hungarians with Czechs, Czechs with Poles, Poles with Romanians, Romanians with Bulgarians — as though they all wanted to pull that enormous, intriguing postcommunist turnip out of the ground together.

I sometimes come across my fellow-countrymen here as well, and watch them chattering about ex-Yugoslavia, about the war and its causes (having escaped from both the war and its causes!), making personal statements, becoming *the voice of the people*, accepting the role they had escaped at home, and are now glad to take on; I watch them adapting, modelling their own biographies, no longer knowing how much is true, and what is a newly acquired image . . .

I look at my colleagues, those sweating travellers, struggling with their luggage: with several suitcases in their hands already, I can see on their faces their readiness to take on more.

'The American market is saturated with East European writers,' an editor in one publishing house told me.

'Oh?' I said.

'I personally don't intend to publish a single one,' he said.

'But what has that got to do with my books?' I said, stressing the word books.

'You are an East European writer,' he replied, stressing every word.

'It's a real shame you're not a Cuban writer,' the editor of another publishing house told me, with feeling.

'Oh?'

'At present, the American market is open to ethnicities, particularly Cubans, Puerto-ricans, Central America in general.'

'Interesting,' I said.

'Have you any connection with China?'

'No.'

'Pity. That would have helped too. The Chinese immigrant novel, that's fashionable now.'

'Unfortunately we can't publish your books at the moment,' the editor of a third publishing house told me, with a note of real regret in his voice. 'You write, how can I put it, "pure" literature. From a moral standpoint it would not be right to publish something like that, now that your country is at war . . . Have you anything about the war?'

'I'm afraid of blood,' I said and remembered that I had uttered the very same sentence several months before.

'I'm sorry, I'm really sorry,' said the editor sincerely.

'But what do you have to do with the war in Yugoslavia?' I asked.

'To publish anything else at this moment would mean

that as a publishing house we are indifferent to the political events in the world,' said the editor with conviction.

Here in America, clutching my books in my hand, my one and only ID (which does not appear to be valid), I am aware of all the tragi-comedy of EEWs, labelled East European Writers, dragging their wretched homelands around with them as necessary baggage, never having been obliged to drag them around until they came here, of course. In passing I feel like a kind of female Don Quixote who still cares about Belles Lettres, at a time when it is changing its appearance, when things are measured by labels, and not content, at a time when Literature is hidden under the names of its producers. Armani, Eco, Toshiba . . .

At a party I was approached by a neatly shaved man twisting a glass round in his hand. I recognized the face of an American publisher.

'I'm told you're a writer . . .' he smiled.

And I felt myself throwing off my whole burden, the labels unsticking and peeling off. I drew myself up elegantly and said:

'You're mistaken. I'm a typist.'

'Oh?' said the publisher with a smile and moved away, twisting his glass in his hand.

Somewhere in a corner, my Literature smiled gratefully at me, my invisible Belles Lettres . . . And I smiled

back and, raising my glass, vaguely toasted the empty
space.

PERSONALITY

I call an acquaintance, a New Yorker, I haven't seen her for three years. Oh, great to hear you, how are you, and how are you . . . We coo, we condense three years of our lives into brief reports: she's finished her doctorate and found a job and had a daughter.

'Oh, you must come and see her! She's such a strong personality.'

This footnote — strong personality — pricks my ear like an acupuncture needle and won't go away.

I imagine a spoiled brat, and what 'strong personality' could mean in this case. The brat doesn't bother me, it's the intonation that gets me. Because she, my acquaintance, doesn't know that I've heard this same phrase, spoken with the same intonation, at least fifty times since I've been here. Which suggests to me, a foreigner, that there are no other people here, apart from strong personalities, and that consequently my life here must be exceptionally exciting.

The idea of personality was not invented by the Americans. The idea is simply a logical link in an elaborate ideological system — the surroundings in which the average American breathes.

The idea and ideology of individualism (as opposed to totalitarian collectivism) implies taking responsibility for one's personal life (for one's own happiness or unhappiness). The idea of responsibility for one's personal life implies in turn the idea of work on the personal life, and the worker is none other than the personality. A strong personality, what's more, which will be able to create an harmonious work of art out of the muddled garbage of life.

In the realization of his life's aim, the American is once again not alone. There's a whole industry for the production of personality working for him. Child psychologists, adult psychiatrists, laws, established codes of behaviour, newspapers, publishing houses, television . . . Everything is for sale, from textbooks with exercises for ego-building to audio-cassettes advising us how to turn a squeaky, unpleasant voice into a deep, agreeable one.

But still, in order for a person to have a personality, he has, it would seem, to earn it, he has to have a destiny, a destiny that will be his alone, authentic, deeply personal. But America rudely destroys one's right to a personal destiny simply because it instantly transforms it into a public, collective one!

What has gone wrong?

In collective systems the idea of collectivism is one of the fundamental theoretical assumptions. Collectivism deprives one of the right to the private, the personal (individuals are subversive). In order to survive, people in totalitarian systems mentally divide their lives into the public and the private. The rational acceptance of schizophrenic duality as a code of behaviour has made them beings of matchless elasticity, *homo duplex*, but at the same time also — strong personalities.

American declarative democracy (as opposed to totalitarianism) seems to have deprived Americans of the right to privacy, transforming the formula *the personal is private* into the formula *the personal is public*, therefore political.

What has gone wrong?

In totalitarian systems the individual has preserved his privacy like the family valuables. What he has not himself succeeded in preserving in the 'house safe', has been preserved in police safes — by the police. The police are as discreet as one's best and most devoted friend. The genre of the personal confession is unknown in the literature of totalitarian systems (the less you talk about yourself, the thinner your police file will be!). Indeed, literature begins at the place where the personal confession ends. Literature under totalitarian régimes has exploited the rich strategies of literary devices, lies — the essence of literature, in other words, and the essence of every art form, after all — in order to express its truth about the world indirectly. With the destruction of totalitarianism the genre of the personal confession sprang into being: suddenly it transpired that our lives were as alike as two pins, and the freedom of confession has destroyed the aura of uniqueness the author used to have, the aura of tragic 'personality'.

It seems that America does not produce anything other than the genre of collective autobiography. Americans appear to swarm unconsciously towards a large police (or psychiatrist's) interviewing room where they will confess their lives. Their very own, individual, unrepeatable, incomparable lives. The role of the discreet police in totalitarian systems has been taken over in the American democratic system by the indiscreet media. The bookshops are full of personal stories that describe the author (male or female) being raped, surviving incest or incurable disease, curing depression, dragging themselves out of the jaws of drug addiction, doing this and doing that . . .

American television programmes have become public collective confessionals: they compete as to who will confess more, better, more keenly. TV-confessionals are like gladiators' arenas in which the fighters struggle with emotions, and the audience enjoys the fresh, authentic bloodletting. Confessions are sometimes produced like real Greek plays: relations, sisters, brothers and children are brought on to play out an authentic family melodrama before the viewers' eyes.

Americans today make public confessions of their personal experience — to order.

What has gone wrong? And what has happened to the sacred American right to privacy?

If you stare at an American's house for longer than three minutes (say, you like the garden) he has the right, according to one of the many laws that sanction the sacred right to privacy, to send for the police. On the other hand this same American will not deny himself the right to tell you his whole life's story at the first possible opportunity. If he holds back, the media will do it for him. Because the private is public! The private is political, so the feminists affirmed, and the political cannot possibly be private, so it must be — public. It is not advisable in America today to shut the door of the office in which you are working. During consultations professors keep their doors wide open so as not to be accused of harassment. In lavatories you are only half-concealed, and your neighbour in the next booth insists on a friendly chat thereby preventing you from having a personal pee. (And since when, I ask you, has an ordinary bodily function which we all carry out been private?) The right to personal illness has also been withdrawn. That is why Magic Johnson briefly informs the media as he emerges from the delivery room: It doesn't! The whole of America knows what this 'it doesn't' refers to. Johnson's newborn baby doesn't have Aids! Even the right to personal suicide has been withdrawn, as the very next day the media will make your tragic, fresh, personal corpse into a collective sociological theme.

America today is writing its great collective autobiography. And when everyone writes there is general deafness and misunderstanding, as Kundera once wrote. America is not downcast, the commercial effect of the personal obliges it to establish new aesthetic criteria: only what is *truthful, authentic, personal*, what is, in other words, *the real thing* (like Coca-Cola) is of aesthetic value.

Will Americans soon begin to wonder how it is that they — who have believed their whole lives in ideologemes about individualism, individual choice, personalness — are so terribly like their immediate neighbours? America, which anticipates all problems by immediately articulating them, in this case too offers its new great, global, protective idea: sacred self-esteem. Work on self-esteem (national, professional, physical, private, sexual) forestalls awareness of defeat, awareness that something isn't quite right after all — because it implies in advance that something is wrong . . .

And if I change the lens for a moment and ask myself who am I, the observer, I am acutely aware that my self-esteem suddenly plummets like mercury in a thermometer. Do the sick have the right to judge the healthy? Am I not sick, a kind of invalid observing the reality around me from a wheelchair with the eyes of a limited and therefore superficial observer?

What is the state of my personal 'me'? Have I ever asked myself that? Have I ever wondered how far I am the product of many years of the fine crocheting of the system in which I lived, and how far I am myself? And am I not at this moment NO ONE, just a number without identity, am I not anonymous human flesh in the hands of the war lords? Because they, the war lords, in my name, without consulting me, are deciding in what state I am to live, in which language I am to write, to which culture I am to belong, they are deciding whether they will grant or take away the life of those close to me, of my friends, whether they will destroy my towns, they are deciding the names of my streets, wiping out my past, determining my present, sketching my future, altering my personal documents, deciding whether they will prevent me or permit me to meet my friends in what was until a short time ago our shared country, they decide whether and where I shall travel, where the new borders of the state I am to live in will be, which newspapers I shall read, where I can and where I cannot reach by telephone, they decide what will be the truth and what a lie, they decide whom I shall love, and whom hate, which words I shall in future be permitted to use and which not. Even my decision to leave the country will not be my own, personal decision, because they will have driven me to it, not even the decision to kill myself would be my personal choice, because they would have forced it on me. So, what am I, the arrogant observer, what is the state of my personal me and what about my own self-esteem? And what gives me the right, from my refugee's disjointed, neurotic, desperate and disabled perspective, to judge a world which is freely setting up its norms, the norms of its normality?

I'm sitting on a bench in Central Park. It's Sunday, it's sunny, I light a cigarette, I smile the smile of a convalescent and watch amazed as Americans run, walk, roller-skate, take their children, their dogs, their bodies, their personalities for a walk. A woman with headphones over her ears, and a little cassette-player hooked onto her belt, comes running towards me in a tight, shiny jogging suit. She notices me and her face twists into a sudden expression of anger.

'You're polluting our park,' she shouts.

I immediately put out my personal cigarette. She runs on, joins another jogger, then they both join a third. I watch the three of them moving harmoniously and personally away, running off into some collective future. The rays of the sun, glinting off the metal headphones on their heads and gleaming like an aura, simply reinforce that impression.

CONTACT

About ten years ago I was in New Orleans. I was with Judis and Hans, writers. The excursion to New Orleans had been organized for us by the Writer's Workshop in Iowa City, whose guests we were. At the airport we were met by a strong, handsome man without a hand, who introduced himself as Chris. He drove us to our hotel and promised to come for us in the evening.

At that stage I didn't know that the strong, handsome man without a hand was just one of thousands of volunteers, members of societies of lovers of contact with foreigners, or something like that. The American came to our hotel and took us out to dinner. During the meal we discovered that Chris was a social worker. After dinner he divided the bill neatly into four. We paid. Then he took out a thick notebook whose pages were covered with the signatures of people from all over the world. They had signed their names and added something about 'the unforgettable evening' or about 'Chris's hospitality in New Orleans'. And we duly signed too. I have contacts throughout the world, 155 names to be precise, said Chris. Then he took us back to the hotel, where we of course exchanged visiting cards. Once I received a postcard from New Orleans with greetings from Chris. That was all. Sometimes I think of that strong, handsome man without a hand. I wonder how many more names he has collected in his notebook, and whether there's any deeper sense at all in his pathetic collecting and in the whole episode. Apart perhaps from a profound loneliness which its owner simply doesn't know how to handle.

Some time ago I attended a literary conference. Afterwards my American friend Norman called me and asked excitedly, 'Did you make any contacts?'

Norman preferred the sacred word *contact* to such words as: intellectual stimulus, exchange of ideas, friendship, acquaintance, interesting encounter ... Or was all of this implied by the metallic-tasting word — contact?

In Middletown I kept being invited by the friendly president of the Exchange Club, asking me to give a lecture at one of the club's meetings about 'the current dramatic events in Yugoslavia'. The president kept calling; the secretary assured me that none of the visiting lecturers had yet refused Exchange — and I relented.

On the appointed day a colleague took me to a nearby

restaurant, the place where the meetings of Exchange, a club of Middletown businessmen, are held. After their agenda I was asked to say something, and I stood at the improvised rostrum sweating and blushing at the absolute pointlessness of the situation. It was crystal clear that the members of the Exchange Club hardly knew the whereabouts of the country I was describing, nor were they interested, in fact, and it was quite clear that I should not be spoiling their lunchtime with stories about other people's corpses. The people courteously asked a few questions, I answered briefly, then the waiters brought the food, and then the president came to the rostrum and gave me a ballpoint pen with the word Exchange written on it. The businessmen clapped, and then we ate warm sandwiches. Later, at home, I stared at my sad fee, my ballpoint pen, and wept. Chewing over my vague sense of insult, I wondered whether there was any deeper meaning at all in this pointless episode with the businessmen. Perhaps the meaning was that these people had in fact wanted to ask me how I was. In their own way. No more, no less. And my vague sense of insult was, of course, something I had brought from home.

One Sunday Norman invited me to visit some old friends of his. It would be wonderful, he said, Steven would come from New York and Frank from Los Angeles.

We had to drive for three hours to reach the home of Norman's friends, a lawyer and his psychologist wife.

New York Steven and L.A. Frank were already there. The psychologist wife was occupied with a do-it-yourself task: putting together a shaker chair she had ordered through a catalogue. The men would occasionally hammer a nail into the chair, discussing whether the firm canvas strips ought to be stretched this way or that. I went out from time to time onto the balcony to smoke, because the hosts and their guests, all of them, were allergic to cigarette smoke. Then we sat in the living room (the wife had stopped working on her shaker chair). Frank, a living museum piece from the sixties, trotted out something about global love, sex, meditation, self-esteem, about a book he was in the process of writing. As he did so our hostess stretched herself over an enormous rubber ball, a new fitness product. She kneaded the ball with her body: first she rolled over the ball on her back, then she sat on the ball with her legs apart and slowly kneaded the muscles in her rear, then she lay on her front and assiduously kneaded her stomach muscles. At the same time she explained the topic of her doctoral dissertation and defended the effectiveness of hypnosis in treating certain psychic dysfunctions. My friend Norman stretched out on the couch, conscientiously preparing a lecture for the following day, and then dozed off. Our host was busy with logs and keeping the fire in the fire-place going. As he did so he kindly explained to me which wood burns more quickly and which more slowly. Beside the fire-place was a manual about making and maintaining fires. From time to time I went out onto the balcony to smoke. Gradually dusk gathered. When it was completely dark, Norman woke up, L.A. Frank had finished his lecture about global self-esteem, and at last someone suggested that we should have something to eat. First we had a lengthy discussion as to what kind of food we should choose — Chinese, Indian, Japanese or Mexican — and then someone decided, because of me, that we should have something 'American' and we drove to a nearby diner. In the little restaurant we ate quickly, and then we parted warmly. Come again, you really must come again, my hostess said warmly. Of course, I said, it was wonderful! In the car, on our way home, I wondered whether this pointless encounter had some deeper sense. Unlike me, my American friend Norman seemed very pleased. He had been with people and it had not hurt. That was the whole point. When I am with people, my own people, in the end it always hurts.

A little while ago I watched a television programme about highly educated immigrants from Eastern Europe. Physicists, mathematicians, doctors, engineers, architects from Bulgaria, Romania, Hungary — they were all attending classes to learn how to find jobs in America. On the blackboard was a message written in large letters: NETWORK OR NO WORK!

Contact, network, networking are words which are part of American etiquette, automatic American behaviour. Americans do not wonder about their meaning, they simply — behave. They collect visiting cards in their organizers, write down addresses, telephone, write thankyou letters, although there is nothing to be thankful for, take your telephone number and do not telephone, warmly invite you to a party, without giving you the address, fall over themselves to come to your party, without forgetting to take your address. In the little dictionary of etiquette, words stick to one another like magnets. The words contact and networking are joined by another two: image and schedule. It is almost imposs-ible to network without an image or a schedule. In the great idea of the image, the fundamental notion is that in the world of the media everything is just a picture; in the world of pictures, everything is, of course, an impression. American socializing ideology offers numer-ous suggestions as to how to design and redesign your own image, how to create a favourable impression, how to increase your personal social rating. The image is a small step on the path to eternity, to myth. And myth is also, we know, only a picture.

The schedule is the organizer: the daily, monthly, yearly or even several-yearly timetable Americans intro-duce into their work, their life and the network of their contacts. Even if he is dying of boredom, even if there has not been a human being on his horizon for days, an American will not leap at the first invitation, but will say: Hm . . . let me look at my schedule. Americans are long-lived. It now seems to me that this is not the result of a general, panic-stricken anxiety about health, but of the simple word schedule. When death knocks at an American's door, I imagine that he will say: Hm . . . let me look at my schedule.

What can I do? I am adapting, assiduously contacting and networking. As far as networks go I've already acquired one. I entered it quite by chance by ordering from a catalogue something called 'The Magic Ear'. What is a 'magic ear'? It's a small rubber device with little rubber needles that you insert into your ear in order to inhibit the sense of hunger. Ever since the magic ear walked into my life, my mailbox has been full of letters. I have a personal letter from Demis Roussos revealing the *astonishing secret* of how he lost 117 pounds. Miss Ingeborg Bach from Brazil writes that she lost 42 pounds, thanks to Demis's secret. Mrs Charrier from France writes that she lost 75 pounds. I am in contact with Mario Tsounio from Greece, Stephanie Presley, Brigitte Barrol, Doctors Hay and Walb . . . I am no longer alone in this (American) world, I am the member of a network of assiduous losers of pounds. As for the ear, I have lost or mislaid it somewhere. Or perhaps, using its little rubber needles, it has simply walked away.

As for contacts, I have made one of these as well. George Fazzino is my driving instructor, my precious American contact.

'Write Fazzina,' George corrects me as I write a cheque after the lesson.

'Why? Isn't your name Fazzino?' I ask.

'In Middletown there are so many Italians called Fazzino that I've decided to call myself Fazzina.'

'I understand,' I say, correcting 'o' to 'a'.

George is a former Vietnam soldier and an old breaker

of women's hearts. Now George is a family man, he has grown-up children, he's about to become a grandfather. George says he studied psychology. As we cruise round the streets of Middletown and its surroundings a lot of people roll down the windows of their cars to call: 'Do you remember me?'

'Of course!' George calls back warmly, waving. 'He must have been a student of mine,' George turns to me, rather touched. He thinks of all the pupils he has taught to drive.

Every time we have a lesson George makes me turn from the road into a small gas station. There's a little café there where George and I have a coffee. George likes the place. The shop changes owners each week. The first owner was Ricardo, an Italian, then Rosy and Mary, and the present owner is a young Pakistani, Amid. Amid is, of course, our new friend. We always have a little talk with Amid about life. We talk to all the new owners about life. Especially Rosy and Mary. Rosy was only 18 and already pregnant for the second time. Her husband drank and often beat her.

While we're in our shop George and I always take a look at the little pond with fish, minnows, because apart from coffee, newspapers and minnows, there is nothing in the shop. That's why it keeps changing owners.

'Are there any fish round here?' I ask George.

'There must be,' says George.

And we watch contentedly as our minnows dart about.

'No there aren't,' says Amid. 'If there were any fish, someone would presumably buy minnows as bait.'

Every time we go to the shop George buys a lottery ticket. He scratches the shiny surface of the little ticket with his nail, and what peers out from underneath regularly is — loss.

'Have you ever won anything?'

'Certainly,' says George. 'Last year I won $50.'

As we drive George and I talk about life: I tell him about my students, about the war in my country. George knows everything, the names of the destroyed cities, the number of casualties, he's angry with Milošević . . . Son of a bi . . . George has the whole world in the palm of his hand, because he has a student from China, a student from Uzbekistan, an angry Philippino student . . . George is informed about my literary problems as well, he discusses genres with me, the role of literature in the postmodern age, postmodernism altogether . . .

'Hm.' George shakes his head anxiously. 'Where is contemporary literature heading, I'd like to know.'

We park outside my house after every lesson. Parking is not my strong point, I brake too suddenly, and my braking makes various bits and pieces scatter all over us. George's car is full of free cosmetic samples, trinkets, little bottles of perfume, make-up bags. That's George's other job, he is a free-lance travelling salesman. He gallantly gives me a little something each time we meet. Last time I was given a present of a whole collection of pills for headaches.

Last time a book fell on us too, a 150-year-old Italian

dreambook which had belonged to George's father, Silvestre. Friends visit George, tell him their dreams, George checks the meaning of their dreams in his dreambook — every dream has a number — and tells his friends those numbers. His friends then buy lottery tickets by those numbers and they always win.

'What about you?' I ask George.

'It doesn't work for me. I've tried so many times, but it doesn't work . . . A jinx!'

Recently George confided his greatest secret to me. He's about to go into the production of cubes of frozen lemonade. The lemonade recipe is a secret, the secret has been passed from generation to generation of the Fazzino family, or at least ever since there have been ice and lemonade. George and I spent a long time discussing the name of the product, and eventually decided on 'Sylvester'.

'That would be right, after all,' said George emotionally.

I have no doubt that the magic of the late Silvestre will work in the end and that George will grow rich. But still, for some time I have been calling ice cubes, ordinary ones admittedly, 'fazzinis'. It makes the ice cubes in my glass melt more quickly and cheerfully.

Recently my American friend Norman called me and, anxious about my future academic career, asked me:

'Did you make any contacts?'

'Oh, yes! Professor Fazzina,' I said mysteriously.

'Fantastic! Just you keep that contact and don't miss out on future ones,' he said.

As for my driving, I took the test a while ago. I failed. *Son of a bi* . . . said my instructor George about the examiner who failed me.

And he was profoundly right.

COMFORTER

When I heard the air-raid siren in September last year, I didn't realize at first what it meant. My neighbours, unlike me, had learned the rules for air-raid warnings — duly displayed on the lift door — by heart, and they knew at once that it was an *air-raid* (not, in other words a biological, nuclear, or any other kind of alert). I let my neighbours run down to the cellar, while I, suspicious of mass phenomena of all kinds, went back to my flat. I no longer remember what I was thinking about. Probably nothing. I waited for the alarm to pass. The next day there was another warning, I sat at my desk, and as I listened to the panic-stricken wailing of the siren I wondered what I should take with me to the shelter. In the meantime the alarm passed. I consulted my friends about *what to take with me to the shelter*. My friend Nenad's mother remembered that during the Second World War, and the first air-raid warnings in Zagreb, she had taken her alarm clock down with her. Why an alarm clock, she couldn't say. But since the alarm clock was the first thing she had grabbed in her panic, she went on carrying it throughout the air-raid alerts. She survived the war and gave birth to my friend Nenad. I didn't ask what happened to the alarm clock.

Over the next few days, at every warning siren, I duly went down to the cellar of our block of flats, into our improvised shelter. I observed my neighbours, they brought some new item with them every time: a blanket (in case it was cold), cushions (to be more comfortable), spades and pickaxes (in case we were trapped), torches (in case the electricity was cut off), radios (to hear the news). Gradually my neighbours progressed from strictly functional items to aesthetic considerations. They cleaned the little wood-stores (arranging them like grotesque, post-apocalyptic replicas of their flats), they brought playing cards, a book or two, someone brought a comfortable armchair, someone chess, someone something to drink. Homes, temporarily lost on the upper floors, began to spring up with unbelievable speed in the cellar, in the wood-stores. The ant-like activity in the cellar during the alerts seemed to blunt or defer that clear, sharp thought: and what if the city really were bombed? Other towns have been bombed, haven't they? Wasn't it all pointless, then? The books, the objects, the armchair we spent days over to get the right colour, and the pictures on the walls . . . That harsh thought moved like a cursor wiping out row after row, stopping finally at the picture of its own body: our naked, helpless body clutching in its hand its identity card with our name, surname and registration number.

I bought my first computer a few years ago. I wrote my first page excitedly and then, probably because of some fault, I can't remember any more, all the sentences I had written vanished from the screen and all that was left in the centre (right in the centre!) was the little pronoun *I*. That tiny letter which trembled on the empty screen, and which might disappear at any moment — were I accidentally or deliberately to press *delete* — frightened me, it filled me with sudden dread. I stared at the screen as though petrified, I felt that I was seeing myself on the screen, from some terrible distance, or some terrible proximity. And as though I were nothing other than a personal pronoun, a single trembling letter . . . *I* . . . I sat there for a long time, holding my breath as I watched my fragile, tiny heart beating in the middle of the empty screen.

Several air-raid warnings, several descents into the shelter with the most essential items in a bag (I never was able to determine what was most essential) *deleted* the notion of home for me. An enduring virus of homelessness entered me. And it was not important whether or not I really had lost the roof over my head. My brain registered the sound of the siren, the picture of thousands of refugees (I could have been one of them), demolished buildings (one of them could have been, and still could be, mine) and it was all stored for ever in my memory. My sense of permanent homelessness has been confirmed by my subconscious which now keeps playing games of building a phantom home, which just goes to show how strong that idea was in me. Or at least how much stronger than I thought.

Here in America you don't buy fruit and vegetables by the kilogramme (as you do at 'home'?), but by the piece. After a few months I chanced to notice that I always buy four of everything here: 4 apples, 4 tomatoes, 4 grapefruits, 4 bananas . . . I wondered why four, why not one, or five, why not three? Then I realized that the number 4 had been chosen by my subconscious, not by me: one apple was for me, the other three were for those closest to me, *the three of them*. My subconscious had correctly set the default numeral 4.

It is only now, several months later, that I discover that, although I came here virtually without things, it now seems I shall have to buy a new suitcase!

The first thing I bought was a comforter. A comforter is one of the commonest words (or at least I happen to keep stumbling over it); but a comforter is more than an ordinary word, a comforter is a means of registering social difference, the cheapest comforters are made of synthetic material and the most expensive of the finest goose down. Of course I borrowed some money and bought the most expensive straight away. I needed warm winter shoes and a winter coat, but I didn't buy those. I bought what I didn't need. A comforter. What is a comforter? A comforter is a feather-bed, a duvet, a warm cover filled with feathers. Now I know that that object, my comforter, was a symbolic substitute for my lost home, that my subconscious had infallibly selected an item that could serve as a mental roof over my head, a protective balloon, a snail's house, a tortoise's shell, an umbrella, a hole, a hollow, a home.

That isn't the whole truth about me. There's something I didn't mention. I didn't mention the sleeping bag (cotton) and the special American button-up bag, which can be used as a cover, as a wrap or a cloak, depending on how you do it up. The idea that someone might see the contents of my suitcase fills me with horror, I'm even blushing with shame right now.

And that isn't everything, either. I didn't mention the bird-box. A real, wooden one. One day I'll put it on a tree, that tree will be in a meadow, and in the meadow will be my house, I'll go out into the meadow, up to the tree and feed the homeless birds. That isn't everything either. I didn't mention . . .

I once had a friend who dreamed all his life about the perfect trunk. My friend B. intended to use the trunk for all the things he needed in his life. B. dreamed about the trunk, about a perfect mobile home, in his mind he transferred things carefully into it, altered the compartments, drew new ones in the air. The idea of the perfect trunk was powerful, obsessive, it was the metaphor of his nightmare, his enduring homelessness. B. possessed both an apartment and a house, but somehow, as though in a nightmare, it actually happened that he abandoned those houses and apartments, bought and searched for new ones, and somehow there wasn't room for him again.

At the end of every year I secretly wish for all my friends and acquaintances that they should at last live in peace with themselves. Of course for B. I wish his perfect trunk.

I don't know why it is, but I don't remember the books I like best. As soon as I've read a book I forget it. One of my favourites is the novel *Envy* by Yuri Olesha. Sometimes it occurs to me that books are like physical pleasure. If we could really remember physical pleasure, we probably wouldn't need to repeat it. It seems that we keep repeating 'those comic movements' in order to remember pleasure. And then, immediately afterwards, someone wipes it from our memory and we no longer know what it was like. *Delete*. It is only when books give me pleasure that I forget them. But I forget virtually everything. I retain a hazy memory of individual episodes, but I absolutely can't remember what the book was really like.

Andrei Kavalerov, the hero of Olesha's novel, stands with a pillow under his arm. I stand with my American comforter. A *podushka* and a comforter. Kavalerov and I are definitely brother and sister, although I couldn't say why. We stand, he with his pillow, I with my comforter, and we smile at one another.

We shall all meet up in Heaven, each with our own

object. Then we shall know for sure which one thing we should take with us into the eternal shelter. But then again, it will go with us of its own accord. We shall all be mixed up there, all of us, those who existed earlier and those who never existed. Nenad's mother with her alarm clock and Desdemona with her handkerchief. At last we shall know who is who, we shall be naked — each with our own object. We shall read each other's objects like a personal biography. There, wrapped in my downy, I shall meet my brother Andrei Kavalerov; I shall glance at his pillow and at last remember the book. Every line of it.

TRASH

'Do you think that kitsch is a typical product of communist systems?' an American student asked me after a lecture about Kundera's novel *The Unbearable Lightness of Being*.

I glanced for a moment at her young, washed face.

'Kitsch is a global phenomenon,' I said, blushing. I always blush when I utter such a fundamental and at the same time trivial sentence. At that moment it was the only possible answer, however. It was the end of the class.

In his book about Gogol, Vladimir Nabokov uses the term *poshlost'*. *Poshlost'* is a Russian word which, because of its wealth of meanings, Nabokov prefers to English equivalents such as cheap, inferior, sorry, trashy, scurvy, tawdry and the like. By way of illustration of *poshlost'* Nabokov takes Gogol's description of a young German.

This German is paying court in vain to a young girl who spends every evening sitting on her balcony, knitting stockings and enjoying her beautiful view over a lake. Finally the German devises a strategy to capture the girl's heart. Every evening he undresses, dives into the lake and swims before the eyes of his beloved, while at the same time embracing two swans he has acquired especially for this purpose. In the end the young man wins the girl thanks to the water ballet with the swans. While this pure form of *poshlost'* merely provokes a benign smile, the other — the one which, as Nabokov says, is 'particularly strong and pernicious when the falsity is not obvious and when it is believed that the values it imitates belong, justly or not, to the highest reaches of art, thought or sensibility' — seems to provoke anxiety.

In the schizophrenic heads of citizens of the former Yugoslavia not only are two realities refracted, past and present, but two types of kitsch: the old type, already long since dead, and the new which grows out of the old, on the assumption that the recipient has long since consigned the first model to oblivion.

Socialist state kitsch has been replaced in the new political age by its own kitsch: what Danilo Kiš once called 'gingerbread heart kitsch'. Both types are populist (because the essence of kitsch is populism), and as their seductive strategy is aimed at the people, they are both above all connected with folklore.

Now as Yugoslavia falls apart (the process is still going on even if the governments of the new states have declared and signed its clinical death), in my split consciousness, along with whistling grenades, screams, groans, howls of grief and explosions, there echo fragments of folklore melodies: Montenegrin, Macedonian, Croatian, Serbian, Albanian . . . The symbol which has remained like silt in my memory is the ring dance, the 'kolo', which was performed for years at all state ceremonial occasions. The kolo was danced by representatives of the nations and nationalities of Yugoslavia dressed in their national costumes. They all danced all the different dances from all the different regions, in harmony: they tripped, jigged, stamped, twirled, bopped as appropriate. That ring dance, the symbolic crown of Yugoslavia, comprehensible to all literate and illiterate Yugoslavs alike, has today become its opposite, a lethal noose. Today, the participants in the Yugoslav kolo are maiming and slaughtering one another, with the same verve, accompanied by the sounds of the same pipes and drums.

The citizen of the former Yugoslavia has not yet forgotten the former, state kitsch, the monumental performances in which the main and only part was played by the collective body. A body ready to transform itself for its president into a word, a slogan, a flower, a sumptuous picture on the stadium grass. The citizen remembers these spectacles, including the last one, dedicated to Tito, although Tito himself was well and truly dead. The anonymous socialist designer had dreamed up a swansong: an enormous polystyrene sculpture of Tito. Then there was a sudden gust of wind which nearly swept the polystyrene Tito away, and with him the live workers who were trying with all their might and main to stop Tito flying heavenwards.

Just as every tragedy recurs as farce, so all the former Yugo-symbols have been transformed into their opposite: Tito's baton (the symbol of brotherhood and unity) has become a fratricidal stick, a gun, a knife, with which the male representatives of the former Yugo-peoples are annihilating each other. The towns and villages through which the baton-relay passed are today being demolished like towers of cards: in almost the same order, from north to south. The collective human body has become human flesh, all ex-Yugoslavs are today merely meat. The fact that some perish as Croats, others as Serbs, and others again as Muslims, does not count for much.

In this utterly shattered, disintegrating world, fragments of the former and present régimes merge, tunes which we have already heard, but in a new arrangement, symbols which we have already seen, but in a new design. In the new reality, which is like a surrealistic nightmare, kitsch has shown the greatest persistence, it was the quickest thing to adapt and come to life again in all its irrepressible splendour. The country has burst apart and its kitsch, part of its monolithic ideological strategy, has also broken up: each side has dragged suitable parts out of the ruins and stuck them onto their new strategic monsters.

Croatia, a Catholic-folkloric variant of kitsch, has re-designed itself mixing up ancient monuments and folk designs, Catholic saints and crosses, gingerbread hearts and national costumes. Out of the ruins of what was once our shared home, it has snatched Tito, who has suddenly come back to life as the Croatian president. He wears white jackets like Tito's (convinced that he is wearing them as a European); hands children apricots from his garden (Tito used to send Yugoslav children baskets of mandarins from his gardens); kisses (in front of the television cameras, of course), lifts into the air and pinches the cheeks of any child who happens to find itself in his path (Tito used to like kissing kids too). In the redesigned state spectaculars the new president is more active than Tito. Whereas he used to sit calmly permitting the people to demonstrate its skills in front of him, the new president takes an active part in the performance himself. At the spectacle to mark the day of Croatian independence, surrounded by young girls in Croatian national costume, the president took part in a pantomime, tenderly placing a ducat in an empty peasant's cradle (symbol of the newborn state). (It is an old custom of ours to put a ducat in a newborn child's cradle for luck.)

Meanwhile, the other, Serbian side has created its monster out of elements of hysterical Orthodoxy, mixing Orthodox icons with peasant shoes, a folkloric yell with Chetnik daggers and bearded cut-throats. Historical periods are mixed up as well: epic songs with the phantoms of unrecognized kings, and these with red communist stars, traditional folk instruments with military bugles, bugles with the barrels of cannon. The Serbian side has dragged the grey suit of communism out of the ruins of what was once our shared home, and pulled it onto their president. In this nightmare of elements where crimes are committed in the name of God, where people are butchered in the name of the struggle against fascism, where concentration camps spring up in the name of protection from genocide — the Serbian president is turning into a monstrous icon with Hitler's gaze, Stalin's clenched jaws, Sadam's greasy brow.

But although the kitsch of today fits on top of the old one like a double exposure, the two pictures are nevertheless different. The declared ideology of socialist kitsch was brotherhood and unity, internationalism, social equality and technological progress. The fundamental ideas of nationalist kitsch are national sovereignty and privilege for the individual on the basis of acceptable blood group. Socialist kitsch was projected towards the future, and therefore had a strong utopian dimension. Nationalist kitsch draws its content from passionate submersion in 'the essence of the national being' and is therefore turned towards the past. The key symbols of socialist kitsch were connected with work and progress (hence all those railways, trains, mines, roads, factories and sculptures of peasants and workers with their arms round each other in its iconography). Meanwhile the key symbols of nationalist kitsch are connected with national identity (hence its iconography of knights, coats of arms, Catholic and Orthodox crosses, sculptures of historical heroes). But both kinds of kitsch employ an identical strategy of seduction.

There is, of course, another fundamental difference. The socialist state kitsch was created in peacetime, in a country with a future before it. This other kitsch, the 'gingerbread heart' culture, is poured like icing over the appalling reality of war. In the nightmare of war nationalist kitsch intensifies its strategy of seduction and penetrates all the pores of daily life like a virus, transforming real horror into the horror of *poshlost*! The sad voices of reporters, long drawn-out TV shots, pictures of dead bodies, burials, corpses wrapped in national flags, the ritual receipt of military honours so like the taking of communion, horrors accompanied by newly composed Balkan strumming, hit songs threatening to annihilate the enemy with folkloric gusto, that kitsch propaganda industry of war — all of this is bubbling in a Balkan hotpot between tragedy and farce, suffering and indifference, compassion and cynicism, terror and parody.

The new kitsch is extraordinarily reminiscent of Gogol's swimmer in the lake, embracing the two swans and seducing the girl on the balcony. We have to add a few more details to Gogol's picture: there are corpses floating in the lake, drowned people, there are grenades falling into the lake, burned houses float in the water with dead children, broken fragments. The essence of the ballet with the swans remains the same: seduction. Our swimmers — elected and self-appointed Balkan power-wielders and their followers — seduce both Europe, knitting stockings on the balcony, and their own peoples crouching, impoverished and hungry, on the shore. The large, dejected, perspiring heads of our Balkan swimmers peer out of the water, paying no attention to the inappropriate stage design. And as always the seduction infallibly achieves its aim. The peoples on the shore, each on their own side, clap enthusiastically, seeing the performance as 'the essence of their national being', as something beautiful, grand and true, seeing defeat as triumph. For, in 'the empire of *poshlost*,' says Nabokov, thinking of literature, 'it is not the book but the reading public that ensures triumph'.

'Do you think that kitsch is a typical product of communist systems?' an American student asked me after a lecture about Kundera's novel *The Unbearable Lightness of Being*.

My student's innocent question precisely expresses the seductive nature of kitsch. We are rarely aware of our own kitsch. It is around us, we breathe it in like air, it lives with us as our daily life, it shifts from the ugly to the beautiful, from the grotesque it becomes the aesthetic norm.

I don't know much about American rubbish. I don't know all its aspects. I only know that American garbage, *trash*, is extremely tasteful. I sometimes imagine America as a gigantic vacuum cleaner, a recycling machine, sucking in everything it comes across and throwing out seductive bales of trash. Trash is elevated here to the rank of a cosmic principle: garbage is produced in order to be consumed, garbage is thrown out in order to be produced anew. Trash is everywhere, trash is the genetic cipher of the human species, as America has most clearly recognized. Its strength is in its indestructibility, in its elasticity, its potential for transformation and mimicry, in its recyclability. The strength of garbage consists in our daily need of it. It is in us, indestructible as fatty cells. You may slim as much as you like, but the fatty cells are always there, waiting for their moment to be revitalized. Trash is expansive, trash has the tenacious character and habits of the desert. In ecology the process is known as *desertification*. In cultural ecology the process is called *trashization*.

Paul Fussell, one of the most lucid of contemporary American 'cultural ecologists', favours a new, broader definition of trash, as BAD. The meaning of Fussell's BAD is quite distinct from that of the word 'bad'. So, what is BAD? 'It is something phony, clumsy, witless, untalented, vacant or boring that many Americans can be persuaded is genuine, graceful, bright or fascinating.' Besides, to identify *BAD*, to be constantly on one's guard, offers one the satisfaction of feeling one is living in an age which 'is teeming with raucously overvalued emptiness and trash'. Fussell will say that a thing which is obviously bad will not remain bad for long, because someone will dream up something and *bad* will become *BAD*, it will be praised everywhere as valuable, desirable.

Despite all the efforts of anthropologists, cultural ecologists like Paul Fussell, 'media ecologists' like James B.

Twitchell, various experts on 'garbageology' (the science of garbage), garbage, kitsch, junk, trash and BAD are all aspects of the same unstoppable process. In the disintegrating, fragmented, democratic postmodern age, which erases all borders and hierarchies, which gives rights to everyone, and everyone the right to everything, through its universal mirror structure, in an age of personalization, a time of the disappearance of the borders between high and low, between art and non-art, in an age of indifferent consumer bulimia, in an age of atrophied senses, all doors are wide open to garbage, garbage permeates all the pores of life.

One evening, driving home from a concert, my friend Norman and I were dumbfounded by a picture that surfaced from a dark underpass and knocked against the windscreen like a sudden nightmare. In the darkness of the underpass was a heap of plush pandas waiting to be taken somewhere. Pandas of all sizes, flung onto a heap like corpses, with faces expressing good-natured black-and-white death — this plush kitsch grinning its grotesque opposite in the dark underpass was a kind of summary, a hologram glint of our global future.

Trash is extremely tasteful in America. If I had to choose between *kitsch*, *poshlost'*, *trash*, between *bad* and *BAD*, I would choose straightforward, unpretentious trash. Trash, garbage which does not conceal its nature, which is unambiguous, vulgar, trash which recognizes that it is simply trash. When I feel like some of that trash, I buy popcorn and the *Weekly World News*, my favourite American paper, stretch out in an armchair and read. I toss popcorn rhythmically into my mouth and devour my reading-matter: I learn that Elvis Presley is alive, the parish priest Sam Beatty has testified to it; I learn that Gary Cormieru has built a submarine in his garage, that Claude Marquezy, a bank robber killed several years ago, now a ghost, is still on the rampage, leaving his fingerprints for helpless policemen, I learn about dead pets which come back to haunt their homes, I inform myself about the Russian murderer who has butchered 100 women and children, about animals which react to UFO signals, that JFK is alive, that the thinnest woman in the world has just become pregnant, that a man frozen in 1936 has come to life, I can learn how to contact my guardian angel, that next year extra-terrestrial beings are going to attack the earth, as the astronomer Martin Stack assures me, I can read about the greatest surgeon in the world, Dr Enrique de Pareda who is blind, about Gary Kosowsky, a teacher who killed his colleagues at school with Christmas sweets dipped in poison, I can be taught how to telephone from one grave to another, learn all there is to know about the death chair which has killed 63 people since 1702, about Wes Haskins who eats 3 packets of cigarettes a day, about the dead bodies of Chinese astronauts which are circling the earth, about all the evidence confirming that there is life after death, about human salamanders, about Ruth Lawrence who grows fatter by the second, about the fact that an earthquake on the moon will in a few days' time break the moon in two, about the famous hermaphrodite Anna Malreaux who impregnated herself and is now expecting a baby, I can read the authentic confession of a cannibal for whom children are his favourite item on the menu because they taste of fish . . . And when I become bored with all of that I can, according to the instructions of Swami Sudhanami Bundara in the same newspaper, simply fly away. I need only to be relaxed, conscious, to visualize myself flying, hold my breath, concentrate on all my movements, visualize my destination and endeavour to stay as long as possible in the air . . .

American television, like a great brain-washing machine, produces a type of behaviour, forms taste, emotions, introduces new topics into circulation. In the flood of new American sensibility, undisguised sentimentality, a new, 'better quality' attitude to life, I clearly observe the way the television model is reflected in everyday life and becomes (for me, at least) unbearable kitsch. In Middletown there is a shop run by Italians. The owner is called Romeo. And everything is as it ought to be, everything is in real-life the way it is in serials about a warm, friendly neighbourhood, where there is a mixture of various ethnicities. And as I wait in line for my mozzarella I couldn't say whether it is this life that has inspired the television serials or whether life has been inspired by the television serials. Everything, as I say, is as it ought to be. The Italian is an impudent, swarthy moaner, gruff and curt. The customers in front of me enquire in simpering, friendly voices what the salad is like today, then tell me, Romeo, should one add basil to the mozzarella, if so, then tell me, Romeo, is this one here fresh, and what about these olives, Romeo, and these artichokes, and how are the children, Romeo . . . And as I stand in line with clenched teeth — I, the angry East European for whom conversations in line are deeply distasteful — a scene acted out between shopkeeper and customer runs before my eyes. I don't know why I experience the scene like a one-act play, dramatized advice on good-neighbourly relations, on chit-chat, like a manual about how to carry on a short, warm conversation, how to establish old-fashioned friendly relations with 'your butcher', 'your greengrocer', who will always select the best for you. I see unfolding before my eyes an exercise in something long since lost, imitated museum emotions, an attempt at establishing something that was never ours, 'nostalgia-exercises', acting, kitsch. And, if I alter my perspective for a moment, what gapes out of my example is overwhelming solitude: both the shopkeeper's and mine, the observer's. And I am immediately struck by the vague thought: is not kitsch itself, in its most secret essence, a call to overcome solitude, a call to a warm, secure togetherness.

'The new Goddess of Dullness is in the saddle, attended by her outriders Greed, Ignorance, and Publicity.

'In short, BAD has gotten such a head start that nothing can slow it down much, even if we should blow up the teachers' colleges; nationalize the airlines; make C not B, the average grade again; reinstall Latin in the high schools; stop demeaning the children by calling them kids and policemen by calling them cops; get rid of intercollegiate athletics; curb the national impulse to brag; raise the capital gains tax; teach a generation to sneer at advertising and to treat astrology with contempt; build bridges that don't collapse; stay out of space; persuade educated people that criticism is their main business; speak and write English and other languages with some taste and subtlety; get the homeless into a new Civilian Conservation Corps; produce intelligent movies; develop in the Navy higher standards of courage and discipline; start a few sophisticated national newspapers; give diners at BAD restaurants the guts to say, after the manager has asked them if they've enjoyed their dinner, "No"; abandon all remains of the self-congratulatory Cold War psychosis; improve the literacy of public signs and the taste of public sculpture; get people of artistic talent to design our stamps and coins; and develop public television into a medium free of all commerce. Because these things are not likely to happen, the only recourse is to laugh at BAD. If you don't, you're going to have to cry.'

Unlike Fussell, I think there is hope. What fills me with confidence in American trash is the fact that it always costs something. Because I'm afraid of free trash. That's the worst: we don't choose it, it chooses us.

A little while ago my American friend Norman invited me to the cinema. Accustomed to going Dutch, I waved my wallet like a sword.

'No, there's no need. I invited you out,' said Norman generously and bought the tickets.

We saw *Fried Green Tomatoes at the Whistlestop Café*, a new, sophisticated product of American soap. We cried like little kids. Norman sniffed on my shoulder, thinking of his mother Edith in Detroit and his grandmother Ellen in an old people's home. I howled as well. When we came out of the cinema, Norman looked at me sadly and said in a plaintive voice:

'By the way, you owe me seven dollars for the ticket.'

Instead of the handkerchief I badly needed, I obediently took the money out of my purse. And I didn't need a handkerchief any more. I was shaking with laughter.

REPORT

'On 20 May 1992, at West 81 & 82nd Street & Bway about 23.00 in the Teacher's Café a woman's purse was stolen, in which there were $200, an address book, a cheque book, a bank card, keys, personal ID papers, social security papers.'

This complaint report was compiled by a weary black woman in a deserted police station (Grand Larceny) illuminated by a dim, greasy light. The name of the black woman who indifferently typed the report, the last that evening, was Jones ('complaint report prepared by Jones'). The person whose purse had been stolen was me. The reconstruction of the event in Jones's report looked like this:

'At t/p/o, complt. states above did approach her table asking for money. Complt. states she gave her a token and her bag was next to her feet on the floor. Perp.

picked up her bag and fled. Complt. able to identify perp.'

What is an event, actually? One person stole another person's bag. If that is an event, is Police Officer Jones's report a real description of the banal theft of a bag?

I try to compile my own report. After all, it was my bag that was stolen. Norman, Madeline and I were wandering through the Upper West Side, looking for a restaurant. It was Norman's birthday. It's Goran's birthday as well, I said. Who's Goran, asked Norman. And while I was explaining who Goran is, Madeline stopped us resolutely and suggested that we go into the Teacher's Café. We sat down outside, a low barrier divided us from the passers-by. We chattered about all sorts of things, and in connection with Norman's birthday we talked about the fact that life begins at forty. I remembered I was about fifteen when I read that sentence somewhere. At the time it had filled me with a vague terror. I don't feel anything, said Norman.

An old beggar woman walked past us and examined our plates. 'Oh, broccoli!' she said, kindly supervising my plate. 'I don't like broccoli. George and I can't stand broccoli,' she said cheerfully and walked on. 'Who's George?' I shouted after her. 'Bush,' said Norman.

For some reason I insisted on telling them about the fact that I had bought some tokens that day, in the subway, at Astor Place station. A Jamaican with an irresistible smile had been standing next to the booth where I bought them. I gave him the change. But some time later, in the subway, I refused to give money to a cripple

186

without any arms. 'No one was giving him any money, he looked revolting,' I said. 'That's life, it's always unfair,' said Madeline. 'It's usually blacks who give money to cripples here,' observed Norman.

Then she appeared, the Black Girl. She circled around like a cat, muttering something incomprehensible, her hand outstretched. I felt the tokens in my coat pocket, the ones I had bought at Astor Place that morning. 'I only have tokens,' I said. 'Okay,' said the Black Girl. I handed her the little pieces of metal, she snatched them and vanished at once.

A few minutes later I noticed that my purse had gone. We stood up. I tried to recall the contents out loud. Address book, keys . . . of Goran's apartment, and of the apartment of my American friends who had gone to Canada for a few days, and which I had collected just a few hours before. There was some money in the purse which I had borrowed that morning from Goran. I had just one token left in my pocket.

When he discovered what had happened the owner of the restaurant did not charge us. Norman was agreeably surprised. For a moment we all forgot about the bag. Norman shook our host by the hand. 'Thank you,' he said. 'That's what we do on such occasions,' said our host kindly.

We went to the nearest police station to report the theft. The report was compiled by a weary black woman called Jones.

Then we went to my friends' apartment, the ones who had gone to Canada for a few days, and rang the caretaker's bell. It took him a long time to respond. 'The caretaker's bound to be a Yugoslav, all caretakers in New York today are Yugoslavs,' said Madeline. 'Serbs, Croats, Albanians,' Norman corrected her. At last the caretaker appeared. We explained what had happened. 'I can't give you any keys, but I'll let you into the apartment,' said the scowling Pole. Norman and Madeline went away. I saw them off and for some reason was clearly aware that I didn't like Madeline.

What is an event, actually? One person stole another person's handbag. And is my report a true description of the banal theft of a bag?

Today, 21 May, I am sitting shut up in my friends' New York apartment. I don't have any keys, I'm afraid to go out. I peer into the windows of the neighbouring houses, I open the refrigerator, I nibble the remains of other people's food, and all the while I feel a little dose of gaiety, I wrap myself in a blanket, snuggle into someone else's bed. I'm afraid that if I go out, if I stir, if I do anything, I shall pull out another thread, I shall unravel the last remaining shred of reality. Because I'm in someone else's flat, the keys of which I've lost, in a strange city, with no personal documents, with no money, which I had in any case borrowed. Everything had been clawed away into the warm New York night by a black street cat.

As I think about the previous day I shake out every detail, as though out of the lost bag. I do a puzzle in my head: I arrange the little pieces of the day beside the

symbolism of loss. And it's as though each piece comple-
ments and explains the next. I read the previous day as
a fortune-teller reads a palm. I reflect on the way all
things mean more than they mean and the fact that the
police language of Police Officer Jones is after all the only
way of describing — an event. Her language confirms
that reality exists. All other language annuls it. And in
my thoughts I rewrite my report from the beginning.

Goran's apartment is like a shoe box. Goran keeps a
camp bed under his bed for passing guests. For the time
being I am the only passing guest. In the morning, while
Goran gets ready to go to work, I stay in bed, any
movement would further reduce what is in any case a
very small space. As I doze, I tell Goran my dream. I
dreamed about a cat, the colour of a peach, dressed in a
pink silk waistcoat. Help me take off my waistcoat, I
can't walk in it, said the cat. All right, I said. It'll get
dirty, I thought as I held the touching little scrap of silk
in my hand. I watched the cat sadly, for a long time, as
it walked away, leaving paw prints in the dust. I'd like
to be like that cat, I told Goran from the bed. Describe
it, said Goran. I can't, I said, in dreams things are wonderful or terrible but they are not describable. Perhaps
you're right, I often laugh in my sleep, said Goran, but
I never know why.

I lie in bed dozing for a long time after Goran has
gone to work. I summon dreams, continue them, stretch
them, draw them out, swallow them with difficulty like
the dry yarn of candy floss. I feel sweat running down
my neck. The din of New York penetrates the walls.

New York is clamped in a vice of 3 'h's: Hot — Humid — Hazy. I ought to get up, I ought to think up something for the day, I have to pick up the keys at five, I have to buy a handbag, throw a few things into the bag. I must not allow the three 'h's to melt my resolve, to transform me into a narcoleptic dough, to rock me in a tropical half-sleep . . .

At noon I'm walking along 14th St. The street glares, the strength of the light makes my eyes sting. Human flesh rolls towards me: faces with a greasy film pulled over them, a broad rear in the grip of a cheap polyester skirt, bleached hair with black roots, fat arms, sweat soaking through a shirt . . . As though caught in an invisible meat machine, I am drawn into the funnel of a sweaty, greasy, dark-skinned race, a race which sells hotdogs on the corners of the streets, which roots among the cheap items in the wide open shops looking for a little piece for itself, a race which drags up and drags out, buys and sells its cheap booty: its rags, clothes which have gone out of fashion, shiny silver sandals sprung up in who knows what corner of the world, neckties, bedclothes, rugs, household goods, food . . . A race which likes leather, leather jackets, a race which for some reason sells and buys leather belts. The women of this race wear shoes with crooked high heels and little chains on their ankles which glint through their cheap nylon stockings; the men often have narrow behinds and gold chains round their necks . . . A race which likes cheap rings: gold chains, gold bracelets gleam everywhere; a race which buys and sells black technology:

video-recorders, loudspeakers, radios ... A race which, everywhere in the world, buys and sells watches, a race which spreads everywhere with those watches, like a cult object ... A race which, even when it's disguised, even when it belongs to a different social orbit, betrays itself because it's drawn by an irresistible sign to stop beside its own kind of traders ... A race which in the Zagreb market keeps repeating in a nasal voice: 'watches, watches, watches', a race which sells cheap drugs in Washington Square in the same voice, the same intonation, with the same dark look ... A race which preserves the remains of its world from total oblivion, a museum race which plays saws, barrel organs and Jews' harps, which dances the Argentinian tango in the New York subway ... A race which sells little magic objects; knives, openers, potato cutters, magical means for removing all kinds of stains ... A race which sells trinkets, hair-nets, balloons, plush monkeys playing cymbals, plastic frogs swimming in dirty pools, metal chickens pecking the asphalt ... A race which always, everywhere in the world, sells and buys bags: big émigré suitcases which stand in front of the shop chained together, in which one can put one's entire life, bags of all kinds, wallets; a race which seems to do nothing apart from buying these bags and cases, which seems to think about nothing but buying a suitcase and setting off in an unknown direction in order to spring up again in another place ... A race which tells fortunes in the street, reads palms, cards, spins crystal balls and reads the fortune of the whole world, a race which, everywhere in the world, does conjuring tricks, engages in sleight of hand and petty fraud, a race which begs, a race which calls out, mixing languages, pouring sounds into my ear like hot wax . . . A race which is dirty, warm, toothless, which feeds New York, nourishing it with blood, filling its capillaries, a race which clearly emphasizes difference, a race which despises its clean, tidy, white, fresh, icy, refrigerated, aseptic other face.

It's noon, I'm walking along 14th St, the one to which the hero of McInerny's novel refuses to lower himself, because he hasn't got a 'lowlife' visa. I walk freely, I have a visa, these are my people, I scent them, I know what they are saying even when they speak Arabic, Russian, Spanish, Turkish, Greek, Polish. They live in the Canal, 14th, Lower East Side, Orchard, Delancey, Bowery Street, in China Town, in Harlem, on the edges of Manhattan, between C and D Avenues, they surface everywhere like moles on tidy lawns, they circulate through the underground yellow, red, green, blue veins of the city.

I'm walking at noon along 14th St, I buy cashew nuts from a street vendor, I eat them greedily, bulimially, enveloped in my sweaty, greasy, warm race. I go into shops, the thought that I have to buy a bag throbbing rhythmically in my fuddled head, I talk to the vendors, they make offers, reduce the price, get angry. I stop beside the tricksters, the ones who spread out in the smallest possible space, on little folding chairs, on a low concrete wall, on the bare asphalt, anywhere, their miniature magician's props: a little ball and cup. I follow the ball, that swift, sponge mouse, here it is, I say, he picks up the cup, the little ball is lying calmly there like a promise, you guessed right, he says, here's your prize, let's have another go. He winds me in words like candy yarn, the little ball rolls, runs away, vanishes, reappears, the crowd sighs, calls, cries, communal sweat runs down our backs.

I didn't buy a bag.
Instead of a bag I bought nuts.
I ate the nuts. I roamed the streets dazed by the heat. I gave money to the Jamaican with the irresistible smile.
Good luck, said the Jamaican for some reason.
I went back to Goran's apartment.
I took my toothbrush and nightdress.
I got into a taxi.
You've got a headache, said the driver.
No, why?
You keep rubbing your temples, he said.
In the mirror I see his grey-green eyes. A handkerchief tied over his forehead, an irresistible smile.
I'm suddenly overcome by the weary thought that I'm growing old.
I get out of the taxi. Good luck, says the white Jamaican for some reason.
Good luck, I say and because of a momentary rush of vague shame, I give him a larger tip than I should have done.

Shut up in someone else's flat I compose my report, I

run through the episodes of the previous day like a film script, I work out the timing, pay attention to the rhythm, calculate the repetitions ... Two birthdays, two irresistible smiles, two handbags, one unbought and one stolen ... And I don't succeed in connecting the story into a logical report. But it does make me think that everything in this world is connected. Even the most distant worlds are connected by fine threads. The sweaty race on 14th St spins swift little balls, covering them with little cups, the sweaty race weaves, draws the eyes of passers-by to the little balls, enchants, deceives, the wily sweaty magicians perform their cheap skills, not knowing it is perhaps worlds they are spinning.

I stare into the New York night thinking that the theft was the legitimate end of yesterday's story, an incomprehensible scenario written in the hot New York day by three 'h's. I think about my black sister. Perhaps she's called by my name already, perhaps from tomorrow I shall beg for money in the New York streets, rubbing myself round tables like a cat. Or I shall do it in one of my dreams. Everything is everything. In the soft carnival New York night black cats' shadows slink through the town, scratching and purring, tying threads into little knots of destiny. In the soft New York night the stars tinkle like subway tokens, quietly pass from pocket to pocket, twinkling like the Jamaican's smile. Black is white, white is black, loss is gain, gain is loss. New York sparkles like a magic puzzle. I let the cat from my dream pad away without its silk waistcoat. Perhaps, as in the old Chinese tale, it was the cat which dreamed me.

Somewhere on the border between sleep and waking a balance is established, somewhere the puzzle falls into place, somewhere all debts are paid.

That's what I think tonight. But tomorrow, in order to survive, I shall reduce reality to the comprehensible language of Police Officer Jones. Because everything else would, of course, be a fairy-tale.

COCA-COLA

A little while ago, on the wealthiest part of Fifth Avenue, Coca-Cola Fifth Avenue opened, a kind of nostalgia shop which stocks Coca-Cola souvenirs. It sells key rings, trash cans, umbrellas, T-shirts, ties, caps — everything of course bearing the Coca-Cola trade-mark. You can buy replicas of Coca-Cola coolers with radios built into them, clocks, toys, dancing Coca-Cola cans wearing glasses, badges, Frisbees, balls, commemorative Coca-Cola bottles from museum-piece Coca-Cola slot machines, cassettes with Coca-Cola music (the Coca-Cola rag, bush, waltz, polka). You can buy souvenir glasses, trays, plates, everything of course in the red-and-white Coca-Cola colours. You can buy Coca-Cola advertisements in all the languages of the world, posters and books: *The Mix Guide to Commemorative Coca-Cola Bottles; Coca-Cola — The First 100 Years; The Chronicle of Coca-Cola since 1886; The Encyclopedia of Coca-Cola Collect-*

ibles; The Ladies of Coca-Cola, and finally, books about Coca-Cola Superstar. You can buy special cans of Coca-Cola produced by NASA for use in a weightless situation. You can read the last words of a certain J.P. Day who evidently said as he died: 'I die in peace knowing I'll find Coca-Cola in Heaven!'

In a red booth in the shape of a Coca-Cola can there's an interactive computer. By touching the screen with your finger you open little windows displaying topics from the hundred-year history of the product. The history of an ordinary drink, which is 90 per cent water and 10 per cent sugar, with a little caramel, caffeine and CO^2, becomes the history of money, business, industrial progress, ideology, the media, culture — the history of modern civilization in other words. In the same year, 1886, America gave the world the Statue of Liberty and Coca-Cola. The Idea and the Magnificent Teat.

And as I touch the screen with my finger and sip the sweetish red-brown liquid, linking thereby into the mega-bloodstream of more than 350 million people in 155 countries of the world, as I drink the sacred Nothing and adapt my pulse to the heartbeat of millions of people, I suddenly seem to see on the screen, in a ghostly hologram, the gleam of a knife.

In a famous tale from the frozen north, says M.B., a Serbian poet whose poem I paraphrase in prose, *wolf hunters dip their double-bladed knives in blood, stick the hilts into the ice and leave them in the snowy waste. The hungry wolves scent the blood from a long way off, particularly in the clean sharp air, under the high frozen stars, and quickly find the*

bloody bait. As they lick the frozen blood they cut their great
tongues and start lapping their own warm blood from the cold
blade. And they are unable to stop until they collapse, swollen
with their own blood. If this is what wolves, which are so hard
to hunt, are like, then what chance is there for people, and
whole nations, particularly ours, which cannot get enough of
its own blood. And it would sooner cease to be than compre-
hend that all which will remain as our only monument and
cross is a bloody dagger.

The lines were published in 1989. The metaphor used
by the Serbian poet soon became reality. The word once
spoken escaped, evil hatched out of the serpent's egg.
And one day, when reality is transformed once again
into metaphor, the symbols will remain, like monuments
and crosses, above the variously coloured rags and tat-
ters on the globe. Coca-Cola here, a knife over there . . .
Pressed between those two symbols — one grimacing in
a sudden hologram flash of the computer and this other
one, a bottle of which I grasp in my hand — paralysed
by the picture on the screen, I stand, trembling. Caught
in a chance flash of two cultures — one which transforms
nothing into *the real thing* and the other which transforms *real things* into nothing; one which appeals to
life and the other which summons death; one which
creates its history out of senselessness, and the other
which transforms its history into senselessness; one
which erects a temple to an ordinary bottle, the other
which shatters its real temples like glass; one which
appeals to the future and the other which recalls the
past; one which waves red-and-white colours, the other

which wraps everything in black; one which seeks international brotherhood by sugared water, the other which demands brotherhood by blood — I bow to the first. The other one grimaces out of the hologram depths with its slogans. *Have a Knife and smile. Knife is it. When a Knife is part of your life, you can't beat the feeling. A Knife adds life. Things go better with a Knife — a Knife is the real thing. What you want is a Knife. A Knife is just right. A Knife . . . the pause that brings friends together. Wherever you go you'll find a Knife. Knife . . . after Knife . . . after Knife . . .*

Pressed between two symbols, between two cultures, one which transforms nothing into *the real thing* and the other which transforms *real things* into nothingness, I bow to the former. I swallow the caramel emptiness, the sweet reddish liquid flows through my veins, nourishing the capillaries of this world. We are connected vessels, we are the mega-bloodstream, the 350 million of us . . .

I leave the shop and direct my body towards Central Park. I feel a sweetish nausea in my stomach, I feel appeasement. The knife which appeared in the sudden flash of my brain has vanished. I walk towards Central Park whispering . . . Blessed be Thou, holy bottle, Coca-Cola, thanks be to John S. Pemberton who conceived Thee, to Asa G. Cander who bequeathed Thee his faith and cash, to Frank Robinson who gave Thee a name, to Joseph A. Biedenbarn who placed Thee in a bottle . . . Blessed be Thou, holy emptiness, myth, simulation, blessed be Thou, Idea, Coca-Cola, Superstar . . . I don't need reality. I'd give everything for bubbles!

CAPPUCCINO

I'm afraid of velvet. Velvet is ambiguous, warm and seductive. At night broken glass makes the New York asphalt shine like velvet. The homeless wrapped in their dirty rags pull on the brilliance of the asphalt and glisten in the darkness like mysterious messengers from outer space. At night the din is mute as velvet. Sounds sleep in heavy iron shutters. When the last one is lowered in the evening, a terrible clatter rends the air, and then all is still again. The warm asphalt absorbs the sounds like velvet. If I happen to be in the street late at night, I walk with great care because in the darkness the world escapes my control. The city wraps round me like hot velvet and I am afraid that I shall stay for ever, grow into the asphalt, melt into it. I'm afraid of velvet, I say. Because velvet is as ambiguous, warm and seductive as madness.

That's why I like the morning. Shapes are firm, sounds

are clear, the city comes to life in its verticals and hori-
zontals, sharp, bright and unambiguous. Like a compass
needle, the morning drives away the velvet shadows of
the night. In the morning, the world is under my control
again. The little square in my organizer determines my
morning path: 11.00 am, meeting with Sally.

Installed in the Borgia café, gazing at the fresh bread
in the little, bright green window of the Vesuvio bakery,
I order my first cappuccino of the morning. I sit, blow
off the thick foam sprinkled with rust-coloured cinnamon and supervise the life of the street. The inhabitants
of the street stroll lazily along it. Dressed hastily in the
first garment to hand, they go down to the first shop for
breakfast and the morning papers or to take their dog
for a walk. The morning sun slides lazily over the
façades of the buildings. Objects gleam in the shop windows: in one a golden horse's head, in another fresh
grass, in a third a tree painted silver, in a fourth a
wooden angel with a baseball cap on its head. A young
man passes carrying a cello, another drinks out of a
can as he walks, along the street come cyclists, tourists.
Workers emerge from somewhere carrying packages in
and out. They all swap and shuffle like cards in the
hands of invisible card-players.

I drink my cappuccino and supervise the life of the
street. Trucks pass by; the names written on their sides
form a moving alphabet: C — for Casalino, R — for Rite-
way Laundry, M — for Miladys, W — for Wellcraft.
Colours dance: strident green, strident red, pink, sea
blue, the green-and-white arrows and red diamonds of

stop signs dance. In the Chinese laundries, suits in transparent polythene tinkle on thin wire hangers, fire-escapes wind round the buildings like black metal creepers, antennae and water towers bristle, trucks and cars chug, bottles flash, fire-alarms shriek, the languages of passers-by pour into my ear.

I drink my cappuccino and supervise the life of the street, I retrace its path in my head, feel its pulse, check the balance, subordinate myself to a mental *walk-don't walk* rhythm. In Washington Square, homeless people sleep huddled on benches, mothers take their children to the park; children, drug-dealers, students, alcoholics, builders, chess-players, all buzz in a weary morning reconciliation . . . Don't walk. The huge, blonde-haired owner of Pandora's Box, surrounded by statues of plaster angels, picks up her telephone receiver in the shape of a pink woman's shoe. Walk. Blacks are playing basketball in the playground, idle watchers take their morning snack out of brown paper bags. Don't walk. Black children clean the windscreens of cars at the corner. My nostrils breathe in the strong scent of marijuana. The young man on the corner inhales his last puff and, throwing away the stub, disappears. Walk. Greasy oil paint melts in the sun, peeling thickly off the rib-like railings. Clouds float lazily over the sky. On top of a building, workers are writing 'Girls Love Boys' with a paintbrush. The brush caresses the letter L. Don't walk . . .

Mentally I take the pulse of the city, I feel the asphalt

slowly warming up, soon the asphalt haze which makes everything possible will appear.

I look at my watch. The hands point to 11.20 am. The asphalt around me slowly steams. I calmly blow the thick foam sprinkled with rust-coloured cinnamon from my second or third cappuccino, light a cigarette, and, there, Sally's coming. I like Sally. I like the two little lines round her mouth that slope sadly downwards. We exchange kisses, she sits down. With her full lips, with the two little lines sloping sadly downwards, Sally forms her words correctly, like soap bubbles. Her children have grown up and moved away, her husband has left her, and at a certain moment everything slipped out of her control, she stopped smoking, that helped a bit, and then John, her best friend, a homosexual, a writer like herself, developed Aids, and then the Mexicans came . . . What Mexicans? Cleaners at the college, first one family came, then they brought their brothers and sisters with them, fourteen of them, now there are fourteen of them, they clean the college, they clean up our shit, says Sally . . . They were helpless, they didn't know a word of English, nor their rights . . . She took it all on herself, all into her own hands, all for nothing, she's teaching them English, now they're all over her, they bought her a Thanksgiving turkey, why do foreigners think that turkey is an American cult object, she personally can't bear the institution of the Thanksgiving turkey, particularly since her life has fallen apart, since the children grew up, and since everything has slipped out of her control . . . In a word, they have attached themselves to her, she is the compass in their émigré darkness, they keep coming, they come when they're down, they come when she's down, there's something warm in that Mexican crowd, but the turkey really got to her in a way, especially when she remembered they had no money, poor things, now her house was full, her life had fallen apart, there was no order any more, no peace, no sleep, everything had definitively slipped out of her control . . . The Mexicans often cried, sang, laughed, strange people the Mexicans, they cried with her when John died, although they didn't know him, John was a god-given talent, oh God, how many people are dying of Aids here, if you only knew, the business with John was terrible, it was hard to bear, that loss . . .

I see the two sad little lines on Sally's face puckering her mouth like invisible pins, she's going to cry.

'How's your novel going?' I ask.

Ah, a strange thing happened, actually everything began when John died. Something broke in her, she woke up one night and half-asleep, in her nightdress, she sat down at the computer, she didn't move from the screen for the next three days and nights, and she wrote the first hundred or so pages in Spanish, and that's when it got going, and she realized that she was not lost, that she would bring her life back into control, that she would write her novel . . .

'You know Spanish?' I ask, astonished.

'No. Why do you ask?' says Sally.

And in the gleam of her eye I catch sight of a dark, seductive, velvet sheen.

'I don't really know . . .' I say.

A chance glance at my watch shows that it is 2.35 pm. The little table of the Borgia café, two cups of cappuccino, and the two of us, Sally and I, are slowly dissolving in the dense, golden asphalt haze.

BAGEL

If I had to choose between doughnuts, muffins and bagels, I'd always go for bagels without a moment's hesitation. Although I admit there's something to be said for doughnuts as well.

A doughnut is a small ring-shaped, deep-fried bun, says Webster's dictionary. A doughnut is a cheap, simple, common American cookie. Variants on this simple puffed dough devoid of imagination, this sweet roll with a hole, this friendly round bun, have taken over diners, American supermarket freezers and fast-food stalls. I admit that there's something seductive in its plump good-naturedness, its wholesome pleasant colour, in its simple jam heart. In order to taste the original model of this creation, the real doughnut, you have to go to a farm. There you can see armies of swelling, tanned doughnuts springing robustly from the ovens. The essence of the doughnut is not only its straightforward nature but also its sociability. A doughnut simply cannot be experienced in the singular, because it hardly exists in the singular. A doughnut is always — a doughnut. When doughnuts bought at a farm are put into a paper bag, the heady aroma of cinnamon makes the purchaser slightly dizzy. At the same time, the bag must never be closed. The doughnut, whose charm is in any case of short duration, lives on air. Lack of oxygen will transform it into an indifferent mush of barely digestible dough, deprived of all appeal.

What can I say about muffins? Webster tells us that it is a small round bun, made of eggs and flour, cooked in a mould and usually eaten hot. I would say that the verbal satisfaction — brought about by the meeting of the upper and lower lips to make the sound 'm', then the slow rubbing of the upper teeth against the lower lip to make the sound of the double 'ff' — is all that the muffin has to offer. A muffin is an infantile lump of porridge, a hotch-potch, a muffin is a cake made by the poor and the amateur, muffins are not just simple, they're crude. They are *nothing* simply by virtue of being *anything*. The muffin is an improvisation, like a child's mud pie, so anything can be shoved into a muffin. A muffin has no character nor consistency. A muffin shows a marked tendency to crumble. Besides, the quality of any food can be measured by a simple test: can it be eaten on its own? Ask yourself that question in the case of the muffin and you'll immediately feel your mouth becoming dry. A muffin cries out for us to pour a drop of tea or milk over it. A muffin has no personality, a muffin is a kind of zombie among buns.

As I stressed at the beginning, out of doughnuts, muffins and bagels, I go definitively for bagels. A bagel isn't a cookie, it's a thing and a food. In the case of bagels I do not agree with Webster who says that it is a small (it isn't small at all!) bread roll (roll!) in the shape of a doughnut! *Doughnut-shaped*, that's what Webster says, which of course implies that a doughnut is older than a bagel, and that is a damned lie! Not only do bagels have a long (Jewish) tradition, but they have stylistic variants in many countries of the world, especially Slavic ones. This cosmopolitan bun is known as a *bublica* in Dalmatia, *bublik* in Russia, *ðevrek* in Macedonia and Bulgaria. And that's just Slavic countries.

A bagel is above all a ritual. On Sunday you have to pop down to the little Jewish bakers and buy a decent quantity of bagels. (A decent quantity, I say. Bagels can't bear solitude either!) Then you have to cut them in half, spread them with butter, and on top of the butter, like flower petals, scatter thin orange flakes of salmon. That is the classical, simple, elegant version. Tuna paste is good as well, and so is the worker's rough version with fresh herring and little onion rings. Such a morning bagel is unimaginable without the Sunday edition of the *New York Times*. The thick Sunday edition has to be spread over the table, the bagels placed on the newspaper (the smell of the bread and printer's ink is important), make plenty of crumbs as you eat, leave greasy finger prints and let the game of the food and printed text determine the path the reader's eye follows.

The strength of the bagel lies in its consistency, in its palpability. Only a fool can hold a muffin in his hand, while a greasy, knobbly doughnut is a tactile insult to the hand. A bagel with its smooth, tight crust, with its firm round body, fits perfectly into the mould of the hand. The bagel fits the hand exactly, that's its natural bed, the bagel is a divine disk in the hand. The bagel plays naturally with the hand, it fits naturally, like a ring, onto a finger: the finger likes it and the bagel feels good too. The wide, dry Slavo-Turkish version — the *devrek* — can be strung on the arm like bracelets.

The essence of the bagel lies in the hole. The essence of the hole is visual. On Sundays you have to take a bagel in your hand, walk to Central Park, stop by the place where the roller-skaters dance and put the bagel to your eye . . .

I look at the scene through the little hole in the bagel. If it's too small, I hollow out the dough, enlarge the horizon. There's nothing odd about it, I'm peering through a bagel, so what. No one gets excited, why should they. New York is a city in which everyone pretends to be a little deranged. Everyone knows that and no one bothers anyone else.

It's a question of optics, I say. Detail, not the whole. The whole is too big, optically indigestible, it doesn't fit the eye, doesn't reach the brain. A detail glides easily to the eye through the tunnel of pink dough. In time with the music a black tattooed forearm glides through the air, a muscle firm as an apple glides through the air, spectacles in a black-and-white frame glide past, a broad grin glides past, skates glide, a leg glides, a gold earring glides, looks glide . . .

Nestling in my little circle, like a mouse in a cheese, I survey the world. No one can do anything to me. And when I get bored, I remove the dough ring from my eye, alter the optics, fold myself up like a telescope. I wander through Central Park, nibbling my bagel: half for me, half for the birds.

There, that's why I'll always vote for bagels! There, that's why I'll always prefer them to muffins and dough-nuts. Long live the bagel! Death to that error of egg and dough, the worthless muffin! As for the doughnut? Let it be.

DREAMERS

You'll see us everywhere: on benches in parks, lying on the grass, our heads thrown back and mouths open, pressed up against the walls of houses, our arms folded under our heads, you'll see us sheltering in cardboard boxes, you'll see us in the subway covered in heaps of rags and you'll wonder in alarm whether they conceal a human body or just its ghostly imprint, you'll see us everywhere ... Sometimes sleep is so irresistible that we lie down in the middle of the path, we don't manage to choose a place, you step round us with disgusted contempt. You'll see us in winter sleeping with our arms round openings which give out sweet, hot steam. You'll see us in the street talking to ourselves out loud, muttering something to ourselves, dreaming as we walk, our eyes open, intently spinning the yarn of our dream. There are thousands of us, we are human larvae, Aborigines, we are dreamers ...

When New York is gripped in the vice of the 3 'h's (hot-humid-hazy), when oppressive sultriness makes the concrete crumble, when the asphalt melts beneath your feet, when the lungs fight for a millimetre of oxygen, when the sky is as motionless as a glass dome, when a heavy golden haze trembles in the air, when the sweet smells of decay waft in from all around — that's when you dream best.

I lie in a bed set up on the gallery. I don't know what time it is. I'm in a capsule, a solitary example of the human species in my own Noah's Ark. The sunny haze ignites the room like an arc light: it dissolves the walls, the iron railings, pictures, books, floor, ceiling . . . I stare at the huge windows, at the one and only reliable signpost — the green sign with the white arrow pointing to the right: Canal St. The gallery trembles. Beneath me flows Hudson Street, where drills have been tunnelling for days now. Drills gouge out trenches, yellow diggers drag out earth mixed with asphalt, old pipes are replaced by new ones. Orange figures draw out orange signs, lines, set up orange fences and barriers. The iron joists vibrate with the noise of the drills, police sirens, cars, greasy beads of sweat soak through the walls. The throbbing from below seems to make the wooden water towers at the level of my eyes rise slowly into the air.

I lie like this and I know that soon the dusty, deserted park on the other side of the street will rise to the level of my windows on the fifth floor and hover like a becalmed ship waiting for wind. Soon that throbbing in the depths will send the nearby police station up into the air, soon police officers on horses will ride out of the police station and trot slowly through the air . . . And then I'll float away as well. Because I am a dreamer. I am an Aborigine.

In my sticky, damp sleep I crawl along the underground blood vessels of the city, its blue, red, green and yellow veins, I turn for a moment into a grey one, towards Queens, then a brown one, towards Brooklyn, and then I slowly rise, stop and look around. My gaze polishes the Chrysler Needle, rubs down the right angles of the World Trade Center like sand-paper. On the Hudson River I see motionless sailboats pinned to the grey-blue silk ribbon like dead butterflies. I blow softly, set them moving and smile in my sleep. On Brooklyn Bridge the bridge-painters have fallen asleep, I rock them a little with my breath, and the brushes in their hands begin diligently spreading paint . . .

When New York is gripped in the vice of the 3 'h's (hot-humid-hazy), when oppressive sultriness makes the concrete crumble, when the asphalt melts beneath your feet, when the lungs fight for a millimetre of oxygen, when the sky is as motionless as a glass dome, when a heavy golden haze trembles in the air, when the sweet smells of decay waft in from all around, I most like dreaming on Ellis Island. I go there and lock into the bloodstream of millions of dead dreamers, they gurgle through me in all the languages of the world, I am a Jew, a Pole, a Swede, I am African, Russian, Italian, I am white, black and yellow. I walk beside a wall with copper plaques set into it and make out with the sweaty tips of my fingers, like Braille, thousands of names engraved in the copper, I hear their voices, I absorb their destinies like blotting paper and — I dream.

As I run my fingers over the Braille letters I observe Manhattan. My gaze rubs down the sharp corners of the World Trade Center, I'm used to that involuntary action. I look around me carefully: Manhattan is as motionless as a becalmed ship. The hot haze transforms the city into a fantastic fossil.

New York is not a city of dreams, it is a city built by us, dreamers. As we dream, we are pressed against the ground, that is why our city has grown so far into the sky. Manhattan is the yarn of our dreams. From here, from Ellis Island, I absorb the energy of long vanished dreamers, those thousands upon thousands who spent decades building the city on the opposite shore. Manhattan. A city at eye's reach. It was built by those who peered excitedly through the windows of the Great Hall, those who, pressing their foreheads against the cold panes, looked at the other shore, those who sat on the huge bundles in which they had brought their past lives and dreamed of a new one, those who had spent months crushed on lower decks and then, when they arrived, had gasped in amazement. Their gasp gave rise to the city. As they waited to cross into their new lives, they sketched their dreams on the sky. Perhaps the Czech peasant Anna Kudrinova exhaled the Empire State Building from her mouth as she looked longingly at the other shore from Ellis Island.

What holds my gaze longest is the glass dome of the

Winter Garden, nestling between the skyscrapers of the Financial Center, the only curved shape among the verticals. The dome is like a gigantic larva. It too is the work of dreamers. Out of the transparent dome of the Winter Garden, as from a gigantic popcorn-machine, new dreams are hatched. New York is a *perpetuum mobile* of castles in the air.

'I am one of millions who do not fit in, who have no home, no family, no doctrine, no firm place to call my own, no known beginning or end, no "sacred and pri-mordial site". I declare war on all icons and finalities, on all histories that would chain me with my own false-ness, my own pitiful fears. I know only moments, and lifetimes that are moments, and forms that appear with infinite strength, then "melt into air". I am an architect, a constructor of worlds, a sensualist who worships the flesh, the melody, a silhouette against a darkening sky. I cannot know your name. Nor can you know mine. Tomorrow, we begin together the construction of a city', so runs the manifesto in the burning air of one of us, an Aborigine, a dreamer, the architect Lebbeus Woods.

And so, when you see us lying on benches in parks, pressed up against the walls of houses, sheltering in cardboard boxes, in the streets, in the subway, when you see us muttering something to ourselves as we walk, spinning the yarn of our dream, do not wake us . . . It could happen that you unwittingly pull the wrong thread and unravel everything: yourself, the streets, the city, its glimmering image grown into the sky, that you pull down the sky itself . . .

AMNESIA

Recently I've become increasingly forgetful. Driven by a sudden thought, I get up from my desk, go over to the bookshelf and then stop. My eyes roam over the titles, I simply can't remember what it was I came for. Driven by a practical thought I go briskly to the bathroom and stop. I simply can't remember why I came. I look at myself in the mirror, I stand like that, face to face with myself, a sudden dizziness comes over me, a vague anxiety. I return, sit down in the armchair, bury my face in my hands. I rock my own face in my hands, think about nothing . . . If I move my head slightly from that position I can see the fire escape through the window, and on the steps black leather boots. If I lean a little further forward, I shall see a young man, my unknown neighbour. He sits on the steps every day. The tenant from the apartment above mine listens to music and, like a lazy cat, observes the life of the street, the corner of Beach and Hudson Street, from the fire escape.

The young man on the steps has no idea that we are linked by a common rhythm. He climbs out of his window, sits down at his observation post and watches the life of the street as though on a screen. At the same time I switch on the television nervously waiting for the news. Every half hour I see pictures of fragmented bodies in the Sarajevo market. The same pictures. Shut up in my temporary New York shelter, in the half-hour intervals between the same pictures on the screen, I go over to the bookshelves, to the bathroom, I lean forward to ascertain whether the young man's boots are still there . . . For the thousandth time I ask myself questions for which I have no answer. I try to think, to remember, to reconstruct everything from the beginning, I try to find reasons. There is nothing in my head but a throbbing pain. Plink-plonk. I try again, by a different, more cunning method: I collect the remains of the ruins in a little heap, I try to remember my school, friends, journeys, cities, rivers, mountains, islands, just like that, from the beginning, starting with my first reading book. Plink-plonk. Nothing but a dull pain throbs in my head. I try again, I try to remember the names of streets, the names of my friends, in Sarajevo, in Dubrovnik, in Belgrade . . . In my memory houses appear without numbers, streets without names, names without faces or faces without names, fragments, broken pictures, torn out sentences. Plink-plonk. A throbbing pain. Everything lies in a grey zone of oblivion, steadfastly refusing to stir.

Viruses have settled in my memory. A fragment suddenly flashes in my head. *The native has a bow and arrow, railway line, village, town/the just keep to the straight and narrow, working till the sun goes down.* A few lines from my early socialist primer — which ought, like one of the hundreds of muddled keys still in my possession, to lead me to some new door, to the answer to the questions — but suddenly they end with the message *Frodo lives!* The viruses in my memory have nice names: *Best wishes, Black Monday, Cascade, Chaos, Devil's Dance, Evil, Guppy, Joker, Perfume, Ping-pong, Sorry.* Viruses have settled in my memory. *Sorry. Not found.* At this very moment, viruses are devouring my country, human lives, history, monuments, viruses are devouring the living, and they are devouring the dead. The masters of forgetfulness know their job. The grey zones of forgetfulness in my memory are completely legitimate: can I reconstruct my own history on a background that no longer exists? *Path not found. Sorry.* Down the screen of my memory slip pictures, fragments, sentences, words, they split up into parts, into letters, the letters slide down the screen like dead flies, they gather on the bottom, turning into a dark silt.

Frodo lives, my virus consoles me. And I go to my temple of amnesia, F.A.O. Schwarz, the toyshop on Fifth Avenue. I go up the stairs to the first floor and stop hypnotized by the *Jolly Ball*, the biggest pinball machine in the world. Blending into the international mass of tourists, I gaze in wonder at the model of Charles Morgan. The mass tensely follows the path of the little metal ball, holds its breath, sighs with relief, sighs with admiration. Switzerland has been squeezed into its symbols: on the model are a Swiss sun, a Swiss ski-lift, Swiss Alps, a Swiss blue train, Swiss cheese, Swiss bells, Swiss cows, Swiss chocolate, a Swiss bank ... I watch the little metal ball sliding, rushing down the streets, climbing up mountain peaks, going into the bank, the post office, the train, stopping — racking up points according to a precise path. Plink-plonk. The little ball shines with a holy metal gleam: the noisy god of oblivion is at his mechanical task.

The hypnotic journey of the little ball pleases me, it soothes my inner nightmare by transforming it, if nothing else, into a regular rhythm. I like the simplicity of the model, that's all I know about Switzerland and I don't seem to want to know more. I like the safe, mechanical journey of the ball. I follow its path with tense concentration, I wait for it to start again. I like that painless, temporary amnesia, that mechanical, dead, straightforward picture. One day my memory will be reduced to just so many elements. No more, no less. The little ball of my memory will slide mechanically along its legitimate path. For a while, instead of real remembrance, nothing but a dull pain will throb in my head. And then it too will pass. It too will pass ...

And now I think contentedly of returning to my apartment, stepping out of the window, sitting down on the fire escape beside the unknown young man in the leather boots and observing my corner, the corner of Beach and Hudson Street.

I go outside. At the exit I am blinded by the sun. An old man, looking like a retired school teacher, is standing by the exit with a rolled-up umbrella in his hand.

'Is it raining?' he asks thoughtfully.

'I really wouldn't know,' I reply.

LIFE VEST

From my starting point, the house on Hudson Street, I start unwinding like a ball of wool. God, I think in the taxi, shall I run out before I reach the airport? I stare through the trap of the taxi windows, in a sudden surge of panic I try to hold images of New York in my memory, I wrap them around me as though I were cold. The images flash and disappear, ripping, stretching, pouring through me like sand. With an effort of will I hold the last scene in the corner of my eye: that place caught by thousands of cameras, where the crosses in the Queens' cemetery merge for a moment with the verticals of Manhattan; they become a ship with the masts of Manhattan soaring above it; set it in a symbolic base, where for a moment Manhattan establishes its symbolic coordinates, its cross. That picture is quickly erased by another, the last one seen at John F. Kennedy Airport through the little window of the aircraft just before take-off. The little grey silhouettes on the horizon look like the buildings children make by letting soft sand pour through the funnel of their closed hands. The picture is so small that it fits into the eye. Manhattan is just the pale stroke of a grey paintbrush on the blue horizon. Scant grey mounds of indefinite outline: all that can be made out are the two small elongated shadows of the World Trade Center and the little needle of the Empire State Building. Manhattan is a fragile medallion, a little watercolour held in the corner of my eye, which will be washed away by my first tear.

The loudspeaker gurgles alternately in Dutch and English. Our brief life in the air is determined by rituals and I follow them in an orderly way. I fasten my seat belt, unfasten my seat belt, follow the little lights as they come on and go off, smoke when the signals tell me I may, read the instructions with tense care, reading the same text for the hundredth time, carefully following the stewardesses' pantomime, responding in an orderly way to their plastic smiles, I take fruit juice, thank you, I drink it up, thank you, I gratefully accept the meal box, thank you, I eat obediently, shift the little packets of sugar between my fingers, stroking them with my fingertips as though they were alive, thank you, I put on my headphones, thank you, I take off my headphones, thank you ... Images of airport arrivals and departures run into one another in my head, one slipping over another. For some reason I remember my return from New York, three years earlier. It was a JAT aircraft, the company no longer exists, because the country no longer exists, the comic wallpaper where your sleepy gaze could rest has vanished with it, wallpaper with little pictures of people in national costume. (Did I invent that? Was there really wallpaper like that in *our* aircraft?). I see a picture of my countrymen shoving their things into the spaces above their seats in the rhythm of an Argentinian tango, the picture of a young woman in fashionable skin-tight trousers with large dots, sandals with high heels, the little straps of the sandals reveal dirty, coarse heels. People shove in cardboard boxes tied with coarse string, they talk loudly, gesticulate, cast uneasy glances around them, they sweat, they are mine, my countrymen. People fidget, stand up, sit down, call to each other, wave, take off their shoes to rest their tired feet, struggle with their luggage in the rhythm of an Argentinian tango. Perhaps I ought to have recognized in that picture of three years ago the massacres of today, perhaps I ought to have recognized today's horror in that confused, sweaty picture, a knife in the back in those uneasy glances, a ruined house in the cardboard boxes, today's fires in the calm smoke of a cigarette. Perhaps I ought to have recognized in that picture of my sweaty, uneasy countrymen mingling in the narrow space of the aeroplane to the sound of the Argentinian tango that sea of refugees now winding its way in sad trains into Europe ... People entering countries in lines labelled OTHERS. Others, a throng of the dark, the greasy, the sweaty, the embittered, the rough, those who cross frontiers with cardboard boxes tied up with string, those whose look conceals misery, loss, hatred and despair.

And I wonder whether, now that these things are so certain, I shall change direction when I reach Amsterdam airport. Instead of the plane to Zagreb, shall I have the nerve to get into another one? Because I tremble at the thought of my homeland. I tremble at the thought of the misery pouring into me concentrated in newspaper articles, in television pictures, in newspaper photographs, I tremble at the thought of the sorrows that have crept towards me along telephone lines, the smell of which has reached me in letters. I tremble at the thought of my old homeland in which I have become a stranger, which in fact no longer exists, I tremble at the thought of its ghost, I tremble at the thought of the new one in which I shall be a stranger, whose citizenship I have yet to apply for, having lost citizenship of the first, I shall have to prove that I was born there, although I was, that I speak its language, although it is my mother tongue, I tremble at the thought of that old-new homeland for which I shall have to fight in order to live there as — a permanent émigré.

'Are you looking forward to going home?' asks the young woman in the seat beside me.

'No,' I say bluntly and I see the judgment in her eyes (how heartless she is, she thinks). At the same time I see her plucking from my heartlessness a sweet little berry, a point for herself (I could never say that, she thinks).

My heart is small and receptive. How many other people's sorrows will fit into one heart? How elastic is the average human heart? How much can fit in it without it bursting? Or does the heart after a certain time turn into a little blunt bellows blindly throbbing out its rhythm?

The route I take between leaving one plane and boarding the next, from gate to gate, from flight towards flight, is a route of inner freedom. I ride along the moving walkway, quickening my pace, with the blue, green and yellow arrows blowing a coloured wind into my face. Then I get off the walkway, stroll around, look at my watch. There is still a lot of time before the next flight. I settle into a comfortable airport seat and listen to the cooing loudspeaker with closed eyes. Would Mr Fisher, travelling to Paris, please come to the information desk . . . Would Mr Ivanov and Mr Popov kindly make their way to the departure gate for their flight to Moscow . . .

I feel good here. I am a human larva. Here, in this no man's land, I shall weave my natural nest. I shall wander from sector A to sector B, from sector B to sector C. I shall never leave. They'll never find me. During the day I shall ride along the moving walkways pretending to be travelling somewhere, at night I shall curl up in an armchair and doze while waiting for a flight which will never be announced. I shall observe the passengers; with time I shall know exactly who is travelling where, I shall learn to distinguish the faces; when I hear someone's surname over the loudspeaker I shall know exactly what that person looks like. I shall live under the artificial airport lights like a postmodern exhibit, in a transitional phase, in an ideal shelter, in limbo, in an emotionally aseptic space. I shall be fine. And if I am sometimes overcome by an oppressive feeling of claustrophobia, I shall not make for the nearest exit. I shall never leave.

'What would you like to drink?' asks the kindly stewardess in Croatian.

'Orange juice, thank you,' I reply in English, blushing.

'Where's the life vest?' I correct myself hastily in Croatian. I blush again because of the stupidity of what I've said, I blush because of its suddenness, because of my unconscious mistake. I had never asked such a question before, and where had that word, life vest, come from, the first I had uttered in Croatian, and what would I do with a life vest in any case?

'Under your seat,' she replies automatically and moves away.

I search for my medallion, I summon up the little picture of Manhattan, clutching it like a straw. It has disappeared somewhere. Words are slowly disappearing as well. I shall change what I have left over at the border like money, into other words. Or some other kind of silence.

I think about all of this while the seconds tick by. For the time being I'm still in the air. There's still some time before we touch down. I have faith in my heart, in the elasticity of its muscles. Besides, the life vest is here somewhere, under my seat.

APPENDIX

Zagreb, 1 August 1992

Dear Norman,

Is there life before death? I happened to remember this Romanian riddle from the museum of communist black humour recently and for the first time it made me think seriously.

'No,' said my mother decisively. 'All there is is survival.'

Here the word *survival* has completely replaced the word *life*. If we can just somehow survive, sighs my neighbour. The main thing is that we're alive, we'll survive somehow, says an acquaintance. In times like these the most important thing is to survive, Mme Micheline concludes positively. Mme Micheline survived the Second World War, the first independent state of Croatia, communist

Yugoslavia, the second independent state of Croatia, the new war, and she presumably knows what she's talking about.

The first requirement in grasping what survival means is to stay alive. And if your nearest and dearest are alive, if you still have a roof over your head, and if you have succeeded in resisting the quite acceptable thought of suicide, then, a citizen of the independent, internationally recognized state of Croatia, you can begin the process of surviving the peace!

'The most important thing is not to get upset and not to eat pork,' says my mother.

After being out of Zagreb for several months, and now prepared to tackle the business of survival head on, I accept her advice obediently.

'Why?' I ask.

'Because people say that butchers have been finding gold chains, rings, tooth crowns, in pig carcasses,' says my mother conspiratorially, and then adds calmly, 'Besides, I don't eat meat anyway.'

'Why not?'

'Because it's expensive.'

People prepared to survive are an odd bunch. Should you happen to end up in a madhouse, it's not advisable to rely on the logic of the outside world, you have to adapt to madness and respect it as normal behaviour, don't you? Perhaps it is just that, adaptability, which makes the people who practise survival an odd bunch.

It appears that a person who has resolved to survive needs identity papers, at least they mitigate the sense of living in limbo, with papers you can decide to move — up or down. After many hours spent queuing for my basic identity document, an I.D. card, I finally reached the counter.

'Nationality?' yelled the clerk.

'Anational,' I replied.

'There's no such thing!' she yelled.

'Surely, you must have some heading for . . . "others"?'

'No! Just tell me what you are and stop making a nuisance of yourself!' said the clerk, addressing the queue this time, exactly as in Soviet handbooks of totalitarian etiquette.

'She must be Serbian, and she's afraid to say so,' commented someone in the queue behind me.

'Are you Serbian?' asked the clerk.

'I'm anational. Undetermined,' I elaborated.

'How can anyone be "undetermined" in this war?' screamed the clerk.

'I'm not undetermined in the war, but under the heading "nationality".'

'Oh, just say you're Croatian and get on with it,' whispered the person behind me in the queue benevolently.

'I can't,' I said. 'As long as belonging to a particular nationality makes one citizen of this state politically, socially and humanly acceptable, and another unacceptable, I refuse to be reduced to any blood group.' I explained my position to the benevolent person, pleased that I had been able to formulate it so satisfactorily.

'Listen, I've got a mate, a Serb, who registered as a Gypsy. Say you're a Gypsy, that's OK,' suggested the benevolent person, insisting on helping me.

'I am — others!' This time I yelled as well, and for some reason reinforced my position by repeating 'O-T-H-E-R-S!' in English.

'There are people waiting, and you're just being insolent! I'll write "others" for you and you can go to hell!' The clerk addressed the whole queue again and I got my essential document, which confirmed that I was a citizen of Croatia from now on.

I'm going to get a new passport as well. And because I sat for a whole day in a gigantic, snaking queue, where we kept getting up from our chairs in order to move one forward, my Croatian passport will be especially sweet. That dark-blue booklet with the red and white (Coca-Cola!) design only confirms once again that I was born where I was born, but because of the long drawn-out battle for it I shall value it as though it were a passport of the state of Luxembourg. Except that, unlike a citizen of Luxembourg, I shall cross borders everywhere as — OTHERS!

Given that I am not a refugee and that I still have a job, my chances of surviving the peace are greatly enhanced. I allocate my monthly salary carefully for bread and milk. I don't pay rent, electricity, heating or telephone bills. I don't buy newspapers, which is no hardship. I don't eat meat. Instead of fruit and vegetables I munch American vitamin pills. I've got enough for a year. I've given my clothes to refugees, all the nicest things have been devoured by moths. I hardly need any shoes, I don't go out anywhere. Instead of cosmetics I use the remains of the real Dalmatian olive oil I bought last year from Signor Bino on the island of Brač. I've learned not to complain. The other day I did open my mouth, and complained to my neighbour that I couldn't buy face cream, look what we've come to, I said, olive oil . . .

'You should be glad that you're alive, that you've got a roof over your head and that you're not a cripple. Imagine if you had been at the front and now you had to push yourself around in a wheelchair,' said my neighbour sternly.

'Heavens, yes.'

'Or perhaps you would like Milošević to come?' said my neighbour in a terrible voice, thrusting her face into mine.

'Goodness no, God forbid,' I said.

'Or those dreadful Serbs to be raping and torturing you now in some camp, eh, is that what you'd like?' My neighbour got more and more heated.

'That would be terrible,' I said, and I could feel myself trembling.

'Or perhaps you'd like us still to be living in the prison of nations, eh?'

'What prison of nations?'

'Why the former Yugo . . .'

'Oh no, definitely not in a prison,' I said.

231

'Well, then, if you think about it, we're really well off!' said my neighbour.

'Absolutely,' I said, consoled.

And for some reason I pushed the bottle of olive oil into her hand.

'Take it,' I said, moved.

'Thank you,' she said. 'It'll come in handy for potato salad.'

I don't go to the cinema, I don't buy books. There could be a bomb in a cinema, they say. As for books, there aren't any, the bookshops are virtually empty. I know that culture is not a priority in wartime, of course, I know, I accept that. Although in wartime everyone likes to talk about culture, about writers. Even our President never contradicts journalists who address him: 'You, sir, are a scholar, you have a doctorate, you're a writer . . .' The President just smiles benignly, although he has never written a line. A line of verse, I mean. For some reason, all postcommunist states like to have writers to lead them. Take Dobrica Ćosić, he's a writer, and Radovan Karadžić, the well-known founder of prison camps for Croats and Muslims in Bosnia, he's a poet and lover of Whitman; half the Serbian parliament are writers. As far as our President is concerned, he does not hide his love of literature. As soon as a writer dear to the régime dies, the President immediately appears on television to express his condolences.

As I say, I don't buy books, there's nothing to buy. In the bookshops there are only patriotic-tourist books and one or two others. I don't recognize the names of the writers. It appears that some of the Croatian soldiers who perished or survived in the battle for the defence of the fatherland were poets.

'We'll print your book if you bring us 140 kilos of paper,' says my friend, a publisher.

'Where can I find 140 kilos of paper?'

'I don't know, that's your problem, you're a writer,' says the publisher.

I sometimes think nostalgically of a distant totalitarian year I spent in Moscow. My friends — painters, writers, intellectuals — lived in happy opposition to the régime, all underground, all up to their eyes in 'samizdat'. What a creative and stimulating life that was! Here, we're all floating around on the surface — some underground! — we voted for a democratic government, we all voted ... And what's got into me, am I mad, what do I want, icing on the cake? I've confused the times, can't I distinguish democratic from totalitarian régimes any more?

I'll survive, I think to myself, I won't go out, I won't see anyone, I'll get harder ... There, I notice with satisfaction that an acceptable crust of indifference is settling round my heart. I don't upset myself any more, that's the main thing. Every so often a Serbian house explodes, what do they expect when they built on our land, let them see what it's like to have their roof blown in over their heads, I repeat the responses I've heard, and I see the approval of everyone around me. Often a completely innocent Serb will be beaten up, but I don't protest, I've learned the words, let them see what it's like to be beaten up when you've done nothing, I say, and I see the approval of everyone around me. No one frowns, no one comments, all nod their heads in unison. As though the whole country, my sweet little Croatia, had turned into a school choir, obediently practising singing in chorus every day. And the conductor is, we know who . . .

I don't upset myself any more, I've decided to survive. I watch the way quiet little patriots move books printed in the Cyrillic script to their cellars, of their own accord of course, but one day their descendants will surely be grateful. I watch the way the name of a school, called after Ivan Goran Kovačić, a Croatian poet who wrote the strongest and finest war poem in Croatian literature, is changed. The school now has a new name, a date connected with the brave defenders of Croatia. We've had enough of these anti-fascists, representatives of Yugo-communist culture, say the supporters of the new cultural campaigns. Quite right, I say, putting my copy of Ivan Goran Kovačić away behind some other books. I repeat the movement, a postmodern reference, almost with nostalgia. I learned how to do that during that year I spent in Moscow. Half Russian avantgarde literature could be beautifully concealed behind the works of Lenin.

I watch monuments being destroyed everywhere: to

Nikola Tesla in Glina, to Ivo Andrić in Višegrad, to the victims of fascism on Brač. On the same island I watch them put up a monument to Genscher. Danke, Deutschland, danke Genscher. I don't upset myself, why should I. Our towns have been razed to the ground, for goodness' sake, and I'm getting agitated about some monument. Besides, it's natural in a democracy that people put up the monuments they want and scrap the ones they don't care for.

'We've always built, that's in our genes. If we happen to destroy something along the way as well, that's not our custom, we've learned it from those barbarians, the Serbs,' says my neighbour.

'That's right,' I say, remembering my decision to survive.

I really don't miss meat. My cholesterol level has fallen significantly. I have grown accustomed to survival, I'm getting quite good at it. It's true, I find it a little hard when I see that life, what little is left of it, has become an exhaustingly simultaneous assault of real tragedies and kitsch. I recoil a little at television shots of the president ceremoniously handing out decorations to the widows and mothers of fallen Croatian soldiers. And they, the mothers and widows, meekly take the little heap of metal, and, occasionally one of them will kiss the President's hand as a mark of gratitude for her dead husband or son! But if I close one eye, I'll survive.

Sometimes I feel a bit sick when I see the mixture of fear and adoration on the faces of the people, such a shamelessly public longing of the herd for a leader, but if I close both eyes, I'll survive even that somehow. I sometimes feel nauseated when I hear my fellow-citizens referring increasingly often to their democratically elected President as 'father', 'dad', 'the old man', quite forgetting that 'the old man' was what they called Tito just ten years ago, but I can handle the nausea.

I sometimes feel a pang in the region of my heart when I see the people beating their breasts with their thousand-year history, and just as easily accepting a ritual, kitsch counterfeit, so ready to erase the years that really were their own individual history, their little, individual life. I find it a bit more difficult when I see the constant crafting by the media of the *state* as victim, when at the same time *human* victims are so numerous and so anonymous. I find it difficult, I say, but somehow I'll cope with that as well.

I find survival a little harder when I see on television shots in which all the participants point little crosses towards the camera, like actors in vampire movies. Men with open shirts so that the cross can be seen more easily, women with bare necks and décolletages . . . We are all true believers, we are all loyal, we are Western culture, we are not wild beasts thirsty for blood like our enemies, the crosses signal frenetically to the viewers. But I'll cope with that too, I say. I'm not stupid, I know what the priorities are. A little cross here or there is trivial compared to the loss of life. But a little cross sometimes reminds me of its opposite: the metal identification tags round soldiers' necks which are put in the soldiers' mouths when they're dead. The enemy soldiers, of course.

'You don't wear a cross?' my neighbour asks me.

'No,' I say.

'Were you a commie then?' she asks angrily. The little cross round her neck accompanies her question with a righteous, golden gleam.

Surviving becomes harder when I think of Jasna, my friend, who is now in Belgrade. She escaped there last year with her two children, when people said Zagreb was going to be bombed — in a word, a traitor. The lives of her children were more important to her than the newly established borders.

'If only I knew how she was,' I uttered the terrible anti-state thought when people were saying Belgrade was going to be bombed.

'I shan't have anything more to do with Serbs,' says my acquaintance.

'Why?'

'Because all Serbs are the same.'

'How do you mean the same?'

'They're all swine.'

Surviving becomes unbearable when I think of the madmen who are still standing at the helm of the shattered ship, of all those terrible, sweaty Balkan power-lovers who have played with the lives of millions. Survival is insupportable when I think of the *individual* tragedies, of the thousands who have lost their lives, those who have been uprooted, those who have fled, when I think of the victims in the camps, of those who have lived through hell, of those in Bosnia who are still living through hell, of those who have yet to come to know it, of the murderers who were good neighbours until a short time ago, of the victims some of whom will themselves become murderers. I tremble when I think of the thousands upon thousands of *individual* destinies, of this appalling, bloody demolition of *individual* lives. Who will pay for it, what new state will heal those wounds, what new passport will make up for the loss of a child, what state border can bring back those lives, I ask myself.

'Don't ask, you'll never survive like that,' says my mother in an unfamiliar, boy-scout tone.

An acquaintance of mine developed a serious illness. I want to survive, he said, I have to live with my illness in order to conquer it. My acquaintance survived, but he changed a lot. He has an absent look, he is incapable of receiving stimuli from the outside world, he spends the whole time holding his wrist. Measuring his pulse, listening to his own heart beating. Sometimes a shadow of hatred passes over his pale, washed-out face. I hate the healthy, he says simply. The state of survival is a state of emotional, social and moral autism, victory brings permanent emotional damage, a kind of insensibility.

Sometimes when I feel I can no longer participate in surviving, I decide that next month instead of bread and milk I'll buy petrol and set fire to myself on the main square in Zagreb like Jan Palach.

'A quotation,' an informed passer-by will say. 'Jan Palach set fire to himself as well.'

'True,' someone else will say. 'What did he do that for?'

And if I don't set fire to myself after all, if good taste gets the better of my desire for self-immolation, if my desire to survive gets the better of good taste, if, in other words, I survive, let's meet in some future life . . .

Your D.

P.S.

I imagine you, dear Norman, nodding your head as you read my letter, smiling, sometimes sighing, ah, you feel you understand it all so well. But I, I don't understand at all. The fragments above were written by just one of my voices, the one that tried to relate everything *clearly* and *intelligibly*, a voice that was addressed to a specific audience (you, in this case), a voice that did not shun cynicism but that was not at all insincere. I feel as though I were breaking up, Norman: all kinds of voices are mixed up inside me and they are tearing me apart. War is hell, among other things because it has a thousand faces which fit over each other like double exposures. I, who still maintain that I am a writer, am multiplying and splitting up, I feel helpless because I have no means of capturing all its grimaces, all its meanings. Reality creeps into all its faces, in a very small space, and perhaps that's why survival is painful. And perhaps that's why any attempt to put that reality down on paper means defeat for the writer.

Since I came back to Zagreb I have been haunted by the same feeling of apprehension I felt six years ago at the time of Chernobyl. I remember that at the time the grass was green, the birds sang, the sun shone, everything was the same, but somehow different, everything was lost for ever. A new age has come, I thought. Later I forgot. Later we all forgot. A little while ago I saw a film about the children who are being born over there now. Pale monsters with one eye, with three penises, with half a head . . .

Here, in Zagreb, everything is the same, but somehow different, everything is somehow lost for ever. A new age has come. I'm afraid that in a few years' time we'll all become monsters. Because war is radiation. And we are all contaminated. We here, who are safe, and those who are living through hell. There will be no winners or losers in this war. There will be only — temporary survivors.

A few days ago I had a call from a friend in Zadar, she teaches at the university there, she spent the whole war year there. Oh, now it's better, she said, we have water and electricity every other day, except that people are dying, they give up and they die, yes, it's incomparably better now, she said, the telephones are working, and the post gets here, thank goodness, except that the postmen are dying, two have died already in the last month.

In those parts of our lands that were under the Turks, especially the most backward of them, traces of enslavement may be seen, sometimes more obviously, sometimes less, and there are times when they all spring up before us at once, in their full import. Then we see that life has been preserved here, but at a price that is more costly than the value of life itself, because the strength for defence and survival was borrowed from future generations, who were born in debt and weighed down by it. In that struggle what has survived is the bare instinct for survival, while life itself has lost so much that little more than its name is left. What remains standing and endures is mutilated or distorted, and what is born and comes into being, is poisoned and embittered at conception. The thoughts and words of these people are never completed, because they have been cut off at their roots, so wrote Ivo Andrić once.

That's where I shall (not) end my letter. Greetings, D.